Letters from Israel

THE MAKING OF A NATION, 1948–1968

Letters from Israel

THE MAKING OF A NATION, 1948–1968

EDITED BY *JAY DAVID*

INTRODUCTION BY *LEON URIS*

COWARD-McCANN, INC., NEW YORK

Acknowledgment is made to the following authors and publishers for permission to reprint the material listed:

From *Israel Diary* by Bernard M. Bloomfield. © 1950 by Crown Publishers, Inc. Used by permission of Crown Publishers, Inc.

From *Letters from Jerusalem* by Mary Clawson. © 1957 by Mary Clawson. Used by permission of Abelard-Schuman, Ltd.

From the periodical *The Light*, two letters by Harold Greenwald dated June 5 and June 13, 1967.

From the publications of the Habonim Labor Zionist Youth and Habonim Alumni: *Furrows* of November, 1942, May, 1946, March, 1947, February, 1949, May, 1951, and February, 1957, and the *Habonim Alumni Bulletin* of June 13, 1967.

CONTENTS

Introduction by Leon Uris   7

Editor's Introduction   11

1   1940's
    THE BIRTH OF A NATION   15

2   1950's
    THE YEARS OF GROWTH   77

3   1960's
    THE MATURE ISRAEL FACES CRISIS   105

    Chronology   179

    Glossary   181

INTRODUCTION

By Leon Uris

The remarkable history of an ancient people, their gropings and longings, their philosophy and religious statement, their fables and magnificent prayers, have been handed down in a work which has no peer in man's literature. Never before or after has the written word been set down more profoundly, more lyrically, more nobly, than in the Old Testament.

We are enthralled by the hairy deeds of lusty men and saintly women in yarns thick with plot and counterplot, by villains and heroes larger than life. We have the record of praises to the glory of God sung from mountaintops so high they touch heaven itself.

This reverence and affinity of the Jewish people for the written word are nearly as old as the written word itself. From the time on Sinai when the Lord gave Moses the Commandments, the Jewish people have bonded themselves to the written word by rabbis, poets, scholars, historians, novelists, ideologists, in an unbroken Covenant spanning more than three millennia.

Once the Word had been set down, it was passed from

generation to generation, century to century, with meticulous care by highly trained scribes. Archeological discoveries of scrolls in recent decades and digs of Biblical sites testify to the amazing accuracy of the ancient books.

After the fall of the Second Temple there was a dispersion that sent the Jews to the four corners of the earth. Some Jewish communities, such as the Yemenites, lived isolated and virtually out of contact with the world for more than 1,500 years. When the state of Israel was declared in 1948, an emigration from Yemen took place. The Jews of Yemen carried out books and Scriptures and Torahs that were verbatim with the holy books brought to Israel from Spanish and other European Jews.

The Jews not only composed and transcribed, but throughout the ages were compelled to go to uncommon lengths to save their writings from destruction.

The first Jewish nation came to an end after a series of rebellions against Rome immediately following the onset of the Christian Era. During much of this time the religion and the religious books were forbidden.

Rabbis and Hebrew patriots hid for years in caves of the Judean hills and in the Galilee and dedicated their lives to memorizing the books and passing the contents on to students. Other scrolls, Torahs, and sacred writings were hidden in caves around the Dead Sea, to be discovered some eighteen centuries later.

Reasonable and responsible scholars of all religions attribute the emergence of Christianity and Islam directly to the fact that the Jews were able to defend their basic writings.

Our passion to save our writings has been dictated by the condition of a race always living with a feeling of pending doom, of being scattered to the winds, or of being eradicated from the earth as an entity. Our history has included the blackness of the Inquisition, the bloody pogroms of Eastern Europe, the expulsions of the Middle Ages, the ghettos, before the word "ghetto" attained a certain influence in the modern American society, and finally, the holocaust of World War II. It has given the Jew a mania to live after himself through the medium of the written word, and the marriage of Jew to his literature is one of his basic characteristics.

This mania reached a tragic beauty in the nightmare of the Warsaw Ghetto, the largest human stockyard the world has ever known. A half million Jews were hopelessly trapped and totally doomed by the Nazis. Jewish journalists and members of allied professions in the ghetto were determined that something of their culture had to survive.

They set up a historical society whose members risked death to collect notes and diaries and any possible fragments of information to describe their daily demise. The collection was hidden in milk cans, just as the Dead Sea scrolls had been hidden in jars centuries before.

So intense was their drive to leave something for the world that the Jewish doctors of the ghetto wrote out the world's first comprehensive study on starvation. Observing old people and children die first, they spelled out their physical and mental changes as they chronicled their own deaths by hunger. This grim legacy managed to give something useful to the world out of genocide.

The papers of this historical society were collected under the leadership of Emanuel Ringleblum and were, indeed, a voice beyond the grave to stir the conscience of all future generations of man.

What more poignant writing exists than the simple diary of a young Dutch girl hiding with her family in an attic in Amsterdam? Through the written word Anne Frank has immortalized herself far above and beyond the monsters who sought to destroy her.

Today an Israel reborn enters its third decade. This collection of correspondence, *Letters from Israel,* keeps perfect faith with both ancient and recent traditions.

Unfortunately the threat of extinction hovers over Israel. I do not believe that this can happen again. If it does, Western civilization will collapse. It cannot endure the moral rot of another holocaust.

These letters speak not of doom, but of hope. They are not the worldly words of politicians and generals, but the aspirations of ordinary people gathered from the spectrum of society.

It is all in these pages: the hardships, the humor, the dream, the courage, and, ultimately, the greatness of man. All those things that make the story of Israel's rebirth an unprecedented event are told by plain people caught up in a flood of history.

It is a chapter that is necessary to be told, for the whole story would be incomplete without it. Future generations must necessarily study and wonder about what life was really like during those electrifying days of the mandate and the wars of liberation. *Letters from Israel* will be read and reread and depended upon as a significant contribution to and an enlightening chapter of the total history.

EDITOR'S INTRODUCTION

Israel is now twenty years old. Although small in size—less than 8,000 square miles—her voice is a clear and resonant one that extends not only across the Middle East but around the world.

Although officially "born" in 1948, Israel has existed spiritually and as a reality for those Jews living on her land for centuries, for thousands of years. But it was not until the 1940's and after World World War II that many thousands of men, women, and children converged on that small Middle East country. And instead of a chaos of tongues and cultures, instead of a Tower of Babel, their hopes, labor, and harmony of spirit gave birth to a strong and healthy nation—Israel.

Through one of man's most personal and expressive mediums, these letters from Israel present not only the feelings, thoughts, and hopes of the Israelis during the past twenty-five years, but those of the countless visitors and non-Israeli residents in that country. In each of these letters there is revealed a new facet, a new face of Israel—and the conclusion that one must draw after reading *Letters from Israel* is that there is no single face or dimension to Israel.

The one—and only one—invariable is the unwavering faith and determination of her people to preserve Israel's existence.

During the past nineteen years Israel has not grown perceptibly in size. But there has been a great growth of a different kind—not measurable in size like a child's growth but one like the spiritual growth experienced by a healthy young adult, a growth in maturity and productivity. *Letters from Israel* not only describes the passionate young adult that she has now become but also evokes her childhood, a time when her Jewish settlements were few and scattered and the threat of destruction was a daily one.

Even during those early years the attitudes about her were varied. Upon seeing a small Jewish settlement in the Palestinian landscape, an American serviceman stationed in the Middle East in 1943 wrote, "To me it was a living thing, something warm, active, organically constructed and with a sounding beat I thought I could hear." And while visiting Tel Aviv, he wrote, "One can hardly convince himself that three decades ago this was all desert. The achievement took our breath away."

This was a point of view based on a brief first impression. Three years later, in 1946, a resident of Palestine was to write, "The land and its people are so new and raw that there has been no opportunity for a mingling of colors—the mixture is just beginning." And he cautions that first impressions are "a false and dangerous affair."

From housewife to soldier, from teen-agers to the elderly, *Letters from Israel* reveals the precise quality of the Israeli experience. Some writers complain of her faults, as one might mildly grumble about one's favorite son; others describe her achievements, and still others her potential. Yet coloring the thoughts of all those in Israel, whether there temporarily or permanently, is their awareness of the pervasive hostility of the nations surrounding her.

In *Letters from Israel* you will read exciting and gripping firsthand accounts of Israel's struggles against her enemies—in 1948, 1956, and 1967. In 1967 Israel survived the most dangerous threat to her life, and in doing so, she took her place among the adult nations of the world. Her growth into maturity had been a rapid one. It was just eighteen years prior to 1967 that a spectator at her first birthday ceremony, her Independence Day parade, had written of Israel, "The whole world is watching it grow with interest. The baby is a lusty one!"

1940's

THE BIRTH OF A NATION

Until she won her independence in 1948, the territory that was to become officially Israel was governed by the British under a mandate ordered by the League of Nations. Although harassed by the British and threatened by the Arabs, the Palestinian Jews enjoyed quiet and intense productivity during the 1940's. In fact, it would seem that as the threats to their homeland increased, their efforts doubled to make themselves self-sufficient and their land productive. These dedicated Jews did not have the time to stand off and admire what they had achieved yesterday or finished today. Instead, their attitude was that yesterday's hours had been too short, with so much left undone today and so much more needed to be done tomorrow. And so the weeks, months, and years passed—and Israel slowly developed.

In this section, devoted to these productive years, you will read letters by both Israelis and visitors. There is an important difference in the emphasis expressed in these letters. Those written by visitors express their amazement and pride in that land's progress; they simply came and admired what they saw. But those letters written by men and women living and working there—by Palestinians and Americans alike—express frustration at the work needed to be done. Their letters are ardent pleas to all Jews everywhere to recognize the potential that lies in that barren Middle East land.

After reading the letters in this chapter, one is aware that there exists a twofold tension—the nagging awareness of how much remains to be done in both industry and agriculture, and the frustrations at being essentially nameless and unrecognized. But however deep these frustrations run, deeper still run the hopes for the future. In a unique way Israel was methodically preparing for her day of independence—but not by any buildup of military strength or arms.

If these Jewish communities had any aggressions, they were channeled into exploring and developing the land's resources and potentials. Israel did not prepare for the day when she would "win" this land—it was rightfully hers—but she prepared for the time when she could meet the world as a self-sufficient, self-assured power, whose own high self-esteem would ensure greater achievements in the future and who could make a worthwhile contribution to the progress of this century.

The letters which follow are as varied in their content as their authors are varied in profession, nationality, and age. The events and experiences they describe have not been viewed through the perspective of time, for the letters were not written by historians or sociologists. Their uniqueness lies in the fact that they were written by the participants in the drama of this small nation's birth.

The following letter, dated October, 1942, was written by S. Aharoni, who was a long-standing member of a collective settlement in Palestine. It presents a vivid picture of the effects of World War II on Palestine. Mr. Aharoni focuses on the critical shortage of labor and its effect on the country's economy. The letter is unique in its description of Palestine during the early 1940's. Also of interest are Mr. Aharoni's fervent opinions on Zionism—opinions that were not necessarily shared by all his fellow Palestinian Jews.

EMEK Z'VULUM
October, 1942

DEAR L.,

Three months have passed since Rommel's armies staged their blitzkrieg in the Libyan desert and penetrated deep into Egypt, almost to the gates of Alexandria. The Jewish community in Palestine has in the meantime managed to overcome the great anxiety of those days and to return to "normal" once again.

Little by little we are forgetting those frightful days and nights, when a Nazi breakthrough to the valley of the Nile and—who knows?—perhaps even to the borders or Eretz Yisrael seemed imminent. Gone and forgotten, like a bad dream, are the mass meetings that were called at that time in Tel Aviv, at which the Yishub's defense against the enemy in the event of his success in Egypt were heatedly discussed.

The fall of Tobruk and the British army's lightning retreat from all the fortified positions on Egypt's western frontier were so unexpected that the Yishub was psychologically unprepared for the great task of organizing its self-defense. Even though the feeling of complete security has been far from the Yishub for many years now—ever since the beginning of the Arab riots in April, 1936—there was nevertheless the conviction, ever since the quelling of the rebellion in Iraq and the successful Syrian campaign in June, 1941, that Palestine was in no immediate danger. But the British withdrawal to El Alamein put an end to all feeling of even relative security. The recognition has grown that the Yishub must do its utmost in mobilizing its manpower for the war effort, and as a consequence of this, the number of volunteers for the army has grown steadily, week by week, ever since Tobruk fell. Were it not for the restrictions and hindrances that are laid in our way and for the British refusal to form a Jewish fighting force of our own, the number of volunteers would at least be doubled.

In war production, too, a marked change has taken place ever since the war came nearer the Nile Valley. Government authorities are much more eager than they ever were in the past to engage Jewish industrial enterprises for the production of war supplies. As a consequence, many factories have been put on a three-shift, round-the-clock schedule, and the need for more hands in industry is further aggravating the serious labor shortage.

The shortage of labor, particularly of semiskilled labor, is affecting adversely not only industry, but agriculture as well. The cooperative and collective labor settlements are particularly hard hit. The labor settlements contributed a considerable portion of their manpower to the British army two years ago, immediately after Italy's entry into the war. In recent months large additional numbers have volunteered. In the past a number of collective settlements conducted their volunteering by means of drawing lots. Every kibbutz undertook to supply a specific number of men, and lots would determine who from among its members should go. But this is now a thing of the past. Everyone who considers himself fit for service in the army volunteers.

The kvutzot have recently given not only of their young. A number of veteran members, men of the Second Aliyah, among them some of the founders of the first collectives, whose many years of service and hard toil in Palestine might well have exempted them from service in the armed forces, have considered it their duty to volunteer and have done so.

The same holds true of the moshavim, the smallholders' cooperatives. The number of volunteers from the moshavim has now reached 1,000—a very high percentage of their total population of 14,000, which includes a disproportionate number of children, still too young for army service. The presence of men from the labor settlements is very marked in all Jewish units. Their influence in raising the moral and cultural standard of the Jewish servicemen is unmistakable.

The departure of so many men for the armed forces has left a serious void in the labor settlements. There are no new men to take the place of those who left. The student youth, which was mobilized for work in the settlements in the course of the summer vacations, was a great help, but it could not very well replace the experienced and highly responsible men who are now in the army. As a result of this, the burden of work and responsibility has fallen on a very small group of people. This has had a seriously adverse effect on the economy of the settlements and the execution of all their work plans on a full scale and on time. Those who remain are naturally working much longer hours, but this is not enough, particularly since in the last two years the growth in the demand for Jewish agricultural products has necessitated an expansion of many branches of the economy in the settlements.

This has placed most kibbutzim in an excellent economic position, and were the doors of Palestine opened today, the collectives would certainly be in a position to absorb at once many thousands of new arrivals. But since, on the one hand, the settlements do not consider themselves exempt from the duty to volunteer, and on the other, the gates of Palestine are practically closed, a serious dilemma has developed. Despite the need to economize on manpower, we must under no circumstances hinder the economic growth of the settlements. It is unthinkable, from a purely military point of view, to neglect the fields and gardens and thus to decrease the much needed agricultural production. It is clear, too, that artificial arrest of the growth of the labor settlements is a grave Zionist sin, for it is bound to have an adverse effect on the future absorptive capacity of Jewish agriculture. All efforts are therefore being made to carry through a maximum program with the available labor resources. Exhaustion from overwork is nothing out of the ordinary these days.

But the spirit of enterprise and the ability of effective execution, which have always been characteristic of the labor settlements, haven't suffered any by the exigencies of the new situation. The rapid construction of the sugar refinery, undertaken on the initiative of the settlements of the eastern emek and the Jordan Valley, might serve as an example. The refinery has been built in Ein Harod, and the settlements of the two valleys are to supply the sugar beet. There is reason to believe that the plant will go into production early next spring.

Even Degania Bet, which has for years jealously guarded its tradition of pure agriculture, has gone in for an enterprise which isn't, strictly speaking, agricultural, when it constructed a number of fish-breeding ponds on its premises. Afikim has led all other kibbutzim in respect to income when it reached the figure of 100,000 for the past year. While the agricultural development of the collective was not halted, the lion's share of this income was derived from its large box factory, from its machine repair shop, and from payment for trucking services. Ein Harod, meanwhile, has begun producing various agricultural machines and implements, including combines, which until now have been exclusively imported from the United States.

The changes which have taken place in many kibbutzim as a result of the introduction of industry could be described at great length. At the same time, despite the difficulties imposed by the frequent blackouts—the sighting of a single enemy plane over the Haifa sky necessitates a total blackout in all Palestine—all efforts are made to continue with intensive cultural work. Ein Harod, by the way, now possesses its own permanent motion-picture theater, which is serving the inhabitants of all the settlements around it.

The labor settlements have but one demand—for more working hands, for Jewish immigration. The cities, too, suffer from an acute labor shortage. Several days ago Eric Mills called together a committee of leaders of industry and economic experts to consider a plan for mobilizing additional labor forces for some vital industrial enterprises. He proposed the training of women for various occupations, such as welding, machine, and electrical work, on the model of similar successful efforts in England. The same Mr. Mills has been for many years the head of the Palestine government's immigration department. But evidently there isn't much for him to do in his old post, so he has been put in charge of the manpower problems in Palestine.

Tens of thousands of Jews are wandering about in central Russia, on the fringe of the British-held Middle East, with their eyes turned toward Palestine, which is ready to receive them and which badly needs them and the productive power of their willing hands. But a criminally stupid White Paper policy—the only governmental policy outside the Nazi-held continent of Europe which imposes legal disabilities on Jews as Jews—has decreed that the gates of Palestine remain tightly shut. Moreover, many olim who have managed to reach Palestine, but without the proper immigration certificates, are still kept in internment in Athlit, even while every one of them could—and surely would —wield a gun or a spade or a hammer in the war against Hitler.

It is bitterly ironic, indeed, that the venerable Dr. Judah L. Magnes should choose this particular time for the launching of a new, liquidationist party in Palestine. The platform of the new party, which goes by the name of Ichud (Union), envisions, to put it briefly, a federation of Arab states, itself part of a wider world federation. The Arab federation is to include Palestine, which is to be neither Jewish nor Arab, but a binational state. To achieve that end, an agreement should be reached between world Jewry and the various Arab states involved.

The dangers implicit in that policy are more than obvious: (a) It makes Zionism and even the existence of the present Yishub dependent primarily on the consent of the Arabs; (b) its primary consideration being Arab approval, the Ichud Party tacitly dismisses the international obligations of the Western democratic world as a safeguard of the rights of the Jewish people to Palestine; (c) it speaks vaguely about an alliance between world Jewry and the Arab states, as if these were equally situated (in reality "the

Arab states" have concrete political power, whereas "world Jewry" has not. Furthermore, the platform fails to specify the terms of such an alliance, or the rights and obligations of the federate Arab states) ; (d) it ignores the Jewish Agency for Palestine, the only Jewish body which is responsible to the Jewish people for the fate of Palestine and whose international status as the representative of the Jewish people has been recognized by the League of Nations and the United States; (e) it refers weakly to a steady growth of the Jewish population in Palestine, without stating to what extent Jews are to be admitted into the country. The platform, in other words, completely avoids the issue of mass immigration which is the *sine qua non* of Zionism. Generally the terms of the platform which concern the Jewish future in Palestine are ambiguous, whereas those concerning the Arab rights are by comparison clear and precise.

It is a pity that our present condition forbids our treating Dr. Magnes in a spirit of benevolent good humor. Though there are few in the Yishub who are not angered by Dr. Magnes' actions, his whole behavior—except for the disproportionately powerful echo which it receives in the New York *Times*—is in reality no more than a nuisance. Apparently it is difficult for a man like Magnes, with ambitions for grand statesmanship and the abilities of an average clergyman or community worker, to content himself with the position of president of the Hebrew University in Jerusalem. The inability to find the proper scope for his great ambitions in other areas of communal endeavor must have had much to do with Dr. Magnes' turning to Zionist politics, though there is no reason to doubt his sincere belief in the political doctrine which he expounds.

Two things have aroused every decent man in Palestine

against the new Magnes outburst: (1) his total unconcern for the feelings and beliefs of the overwhelming majority of the Yishub, who consider his policy harmful to the interests of Zionism, and his complete disregard of the Jewish masses in the Galut, from whom he might properly have inquired whether they are willing to forfeit their right to Palestine; and (2) the orientation of Dr. Magnes precisely toward those Arab elements which are the mortal enemies not only of political Zionism, but even of the small Jewish population already in Palestine.

Dr. Magnes has surrounded himself with a group of men who wield little influence in the Yishub. Were it not that we are living in a political volcano, we could well afford to ignore him and his utterances altogether. But we are still weak, our life and our future are still in great danger, and even a phenomenon like Dr. Magnes can cause us great harm under certain conditions. Preaching peace with the Arabs, at the price of concessions, which include a curtailment or even a stoppage of Jewish immigration, while Palestine remains the only haven for millions of homeless and shelterless Jews and when the country is in such desperate need of additional working hands, is an unpardonable provocation. We are living in the hope that not only the Yishub but the Zionist movement in the free countries will find a suitable answer to the damaging activities of Dr. Magnes and his companions. . . .

With best regards,

S.

Written in 1946 by Herb Weiner, an American student at the Hebrew University on Mount Scopus, this letter is an ardent articulation of what the writer feels is Palestine's need: more Americans. Mr. Weiner describes the potential and strength of the land and its people—qualities that would become dramatically evident in the decades to follow.

1946

DEAR K AND A:

I herewith begin my correspondence with America in earnest and without apologies for time lost. I've deliberately, until now, refrained from writing freely, and the reason is not laziness alone. A letter from Palestine is a responsible creation with power to build or destroy, to inspire or to deflate. It isn't enough to jot down your impressions, for affairs and feelings are at stake which are more important than your own particular impressions. So I've been waiting for things to soak in, and I've tried to expose myself to more than localized conditions of shadow and light. This well-rounded exposure is important here. The land and its people are so new and raw that there has been no opportunity for a mingling of colors—the mixture is just beginning. This "rawness," added to the natural contrast of geography, climate, and people with which Palestine is so full, goes to make first impressions a false and dangerous affair. One can just happen to spend his time in an area of shadow for quite a while without even becoming aware of a close-by area of light—for as I said, interpenetration and mixture are but beginning. City and kibbutz, and even kibbutz and kibbutz are sometimes different worlds, and the general mold and character of the country and its people are still divided into almost untouching fragments.

Now that I want to write—where to begin? First about the Americans here. The bunch that has come on the first three or four boats is really composed of wonderful stuff. A good portion of them are intent on staying, and almost all of them are healthy spirited high-class representatives of American Jewry. It's hard to exaggerate the eagerness—almost reverence—with which they are received in Palestine. They are looked upon as clean-cut and undaunted by Galut. They are considered no less courageous and fine than the sabras and much more intelligent. Into this exaggerated opinion are nursed a lot of impressions which are received at the cinema, plus a lot of judgments which are made because the Palestinian wants to be so. In a sense they are looked on as the products of those conditions, wealth, education, culture, etc., which the Palestinian feels to be lacking in his country. With it all are mixed a certain amount of resentment and a dash of scorn at the spoiled quality of American Jewry and their money Zionism, but it's not very convincing. In short, the country is crying out for Americans. More than once in the kibbutz, after a new batch of refugees decide to quit the life and try their luck in the city, I've heard the words *"Eyn davar, od me-at nekabel kvutza breeach shel Amerikanim* [Never mind, we'll soon receive a healthy group of Americans]."

But not only the kibbutz—every door in the country opens at the magic sound—American! The land is full of strangers, but the only one who can walk into the hospital to visit at the wrong hour or have a bus stop for him at the wrong station is an American. What do you make of it? Well, I'm coming to the decision that their opinion of American Jewry is certainly naïve. They need American

Jews here in the worst way. Of course, the bunch that is here now is particularly fine material. The health and the life they bring with their presence are amazing. Whether it be at the university or at a kibbutz, they radiate strength, optimism, and idealism—the people here feel it and want more.

Let's face the facts. There is no better human material than the aliyah which came here from East Europe before Hitler. But they're on in years now, years filled with wearisome and often unending fight, and the future is still as uncertain as ever. Of the aliyah since Hitler—some have become wonderful material, but significant proportions of it have remained energyless, filled with memories of the past and oblivious to the deeper meanings of Zionism.

And the sabras—they are a book in themselves. One of the shadows, or what to me appeared to be a shadow, because after better acquaintance I'm beginning to change my mind, is the sabra. He is the symbol of bravery and health without par in the world. Those who have wanted Zionism so that *niyeh kechol hagoyim* [we shall be like all people] have almost got their wish. He is a new type of Jew, without complexes and burning intellectual gyration, uncomplicated by inner dilemmas. He is a fine Palestinian patriot ready to give his life for his fellow Jew in any part of the world. But in spite of this idealism, he is without the vision and soul of his father. Palestine is his country, and he will work and fight for it; but missing are the nuances and meanings and depths which his father felt to exist in his vision of a Jewish homeland. In short, the sabra is a patriot like the patriots of every land. But to the growing dismay of his father, he is pretty oblivious to that tremendous history and its heritage which 'til now have made us more than just "patriots" or just "a people" like others.

But as someone remarked the other day, a country creates the type of person who can best live in it, build it, and the sabra, not the complicated intellectual, is what is needed now in the period of creation. Perhaps this is true, but there still remains a great need for elements which are not only healthy in body, but alive, eager, and growing in mind, too. There still remains the need for an element which will watch over and hand down those conquests of spirit which our people have made at the cost of so much blood through the years. Americans can be part of that element. I'm not speaking now only of the Jewish heritage. Even Americans without Jewish backgrounds have a great contribution to make. They are products of a fine and high culture; they are educated; they have contact with and knowledge of a fine civilization. Palestine and the native Palestinian needs this; Hebrew nationalist that he is, son of the deepest-rooted culture in the world, he has not partaken of it. Having rejected the whole religious pattern, he has not yet found any other pattern to take its place. The result is a step downward in the cultural level of his life.

I don't mean to romanticize American Jewry and its culture—I know its emptiness and its faults—but it does have virtues and these virtues Palestine needs. Of course, what relation all this has to the present reality and possibility of an American aliyah, I don't know. But I write these things because I know that they are opinions entirely different from those that I possessed while in the United States.

The weather in Palestine—at least in Jerusalem—is the most wonderful in the world, and don't let anybody tell you different. It's really a lovely country, with clear skies, deep, sullen valleys, and steep, rising slopes. And as you look about and breathe in the air, all the little shadows seem to fade. And then you meet the miracle which you can never really get used to. Little children, beautiful and straight, run around, play and fight with each other, and everything that comes out of their mouths is Hebrew. It's silly, but you can't get over the thrill of hearing a child speaking his natural tongue in Palestine. And the elders, too, do remarkably well, though the naturalness is lacking. Yet the gigantic accomplishment of a language reborn is before you and is solidly impressed.

Regards,
HERB

During the critical period before the war of independence, life on a kibbutz held many harrowing experiences. The threat of an attack by Arabs was ever-present, and in their fight for survival the Israelis often had to outsmart their foes. The following letter, written by David Bleviss in 1947, describes in detail such an incident.

HAMADIA
December, 1947

DEAR M. B.,

I had an interesting experience this morning. Last night I was informed that I was to be shomer hamayim. I thought it was to be a little job in the field for this morning. Well, I awoke at 3:45 A.M. and went to the kitchen to snatch something to eat and met my partner. I ate two slices of salami fried in an egg. My partner turned out to be partners—five of them. I donned a uniform of the Palestine Jewish Police, received a Canadian-made rifle, and loaded my pockets with two hand grenades. You should have seen the collection of arms—two were carrying Stens; all had grenades; three, in addition to rifles, had revolvers. . . .

It was still very dark when we tramped out past the gate in silence in single file. Cigarettes were passed out, and we were on our way. Our job was a simple one. It was our turn to have the water running in a channel which is used by Arabs the rest of the week. We simply had to close the various branches used by the Arabs. The purpose of all this protection was that we do our work at the foot of the hills just below the Arab village of Bet Shan.

We walked for two kilometers or so, often dropping to our knees when a warning signal was given. When we reached the road, we crossed singly, waiting our turns. When we reached our destination, one fellow began throwing rocks into the water to dam it and thus channel it toward Hamadia. One guard stood next to him with his rifle ready. I and three others crouched in the bushes, each facing a different direction. So the work went on—setting up one dam after another. After two hours we were through. Day was breaking as we trudged home. When I arrived, I threw off my uniform and put the arms away. A morning's work was done. Then I went to clean the barn of manure. . . .

Best wishes,
DAVID BLEVISS

Corporal Irving Gerowitz, in a letter to relatives written in 1943, describes a trip he took through Palestine. He writes about the landscape and the cities of Jerusalem and Tel Aviv. Corporal Gerowitz expresses amazement at the growth and development of this once barren land. Yet in the following two decades the entire world was astonished that such a small and new nation could develop with such intensity and swiftness.

1943

DEAR L.,

Time passes very quickly in this man's army, and little did I realize that so much time has elapsed between this writing and the trip I took that memorable week in April. And so perforce I must tell you rather hastily but not completely of what I have learned during my very short stay in the Biblical land.

We all began to feel impatient as the train showed little indication of pulling out. But suddenly there came a jerk; yes, it was the train that moved and grunted, gave a warning whistle, and we were off to a new adventure. In my mind began to churn the books and stuff I have read about the Holy Land, the days of the Bible, the First World War, the stories of Allenby and Lawrence, and now something different, a constructive achievement, an era and epoch I have read about but was not yet to witness. Thus my mind raced, and thus was I carried away steeped in thought until the train made the first of its many frequent stops. We had stopped in a small village, were besieged by small children, natives, cadging out their existence, scrambling and quarreling for the few coins thrown out for them. This scene need not be dwelt on, for its social manifestations are apparent enough. And as the train began to move again, I knew I had seen something unerasable. Before me was epitomized the medieval ages. Humanity at low ebb. I knew immediately that here were the people of the desert that never knew anything but the desert, living by their wits on a barren soil where life expectancy was no more than that of a horse. And as night came, we saw camps of these nomadic tribes dimly illuminated by fire. There they lived; there they roamed as they did thousands of years ago. I could hardly believe it. For the first time I was fully conscious that a little beyond was another world. We were traveling third class, our seats were getting calloused, weariness was becoming overbearing, and as I closed my eyes to find solace in sleep, I smiled in anticipation of tomorrow's dawn.

Morning finally came, and broken as I was, I tried immediately to fix my eyes on the passing landscape. As things came into focus, I saw that we were passing the mountainous parts of the country. Palestine, as I knew, was a very mountainous country, and as such, I hardly lost track of them during my three and one-half days' stay. Everywhere a mountain was found protruding from the mother earth it was bedecked with a natural beauty that invited examination. In many places we found mountains cultivated in ledges which only added to their stately beauty. Everywhere was to be seen intensive agricultural activity. To be sure, in many instances the means of cultivation was primitive—at least, hardly comparable to the mechanization of American farming—but it can be readily understood that the fast influx of the past two decades has perforce made agriculture profitable, notwithstanding the means employed for its end.

Suddenly my eye caught the first Jewish settlement! I looked not intently, rather with bewilderment, and possessed a strange feeling that the train would stop for me and that I would walk down the slope, for the settlement rested in a valley, and I would shake its hand. This personification is not too fantastic to grasp. To me it was a living thing, something warm, active, organically constructed, and with a sounding beat I thought I could hear. There it was, trim and smug and indeed a far cry from the desert we had left the day before. But regardless of my very strong desire, the train moved on, and my disappointment was keenly felt.

We were heading for Jerusalem, and it was inevitable, despite the slowness of the train, that we arrive at our destination. Mount Scopus was our first stop. I inspected the Hebrew University, and the Hadassah Hospital, the nurses' training quarters, where I made some exceedingly interesting observations (as you may have expected from me). From this perch I saw a good deal of Jerusalem. Briefly, it was wonderful to gaze from this summit at a city part new and part old—a city I never in my life expected to see. From there we went to the walled-in Old City. We visited the Arab and Jewish quarters, saw King David's Tower, the Wailing Wall, the oldest Jewish synagogue in Jerusalem. In this narrow little world, in other than the physical sense, we were often forced to hug the walls of its very narrow streets when herds of goats or sheep were driven home from their pasture and often by six-year-old shepherds. Antiquity is always phenomenal, and the legends of the respective sights I visited left me weak with wonderment, but its living occupants left me equally as weak.

We visited a very famous structure in Jewish life. Indeed, a very substantial edifice—the Home of the Jewish National Fund, or Keren Kayemeth. Here we inspected the exact replica of Theodor Herzl's study. That is a story by itself. One hour in this room, and you feel as though you knew this great personality. We inspected the golden books in which were inscribed notable contributions to the fund, and also juvenile books that had even photographs of the young contributors. Two and one-half hours after we first entered this most symbolic structure, we were off to Tel Aviv. There, time was short. But withal, I managed to see the port that experts claimed could not be built, and my own father has now had his faith substantiated for the support he has given it. We rode a bus on a short inspection tour. One can hardly convince himself that three decades ago this was all desert. The achievement took our breath away. Yet there was so much to remain unseen. I departed reluctantly, but within me the firm resolve that I must return for a more detailed examination. At this time it is not yet possible; but conditions change, and there lies hope.

Regards to all,
IRVING

Received in 1946 by a Palestinian living in America, the following letter was written by a young man who arrived in Israel during 1945. The author, among thousands, was a member of the group that recaptured the collective settlement at Birya, near Safed. The kibbutz had been forcibly evacuated by the Palestine administration.

DEGANIA BET
Spring, 1946

DEAR M.,

. . . The Palestine Yishub decided to resettle the kibbutz at Birya on a heroic day in our history—the anniversary of the death in battle at Tel Hai of Joseph Trumpeldor and his comrades. Seventy-five men started out from Degania on the way to Birya. In the afternoon we arrived in Kvutza X in the Galilee. A group of 800 men and women from all corners of the land had gathered there. In the evening we embarked on our mission: to rebuild Birya. We were to take our positions at a spot 500 meters from the place where the military were now encamped, and we were to carry out our task under all conditions, in any sort of weather. By 1 o'clock in the morning we were on our way— a long chain of men and women burdened down like mules with suitcases, tent canvasses, building tools, barracks parts.

For four hours we climbed and struggled along a narrow and dangerous path, in the rain and wind, over cliffs and through water. But we were going gladly. Finally, we arrived. Nine hundred meters above sea level. A wonderful view of the Huleh Valley and Lake Kinneret. There was a strong wind. Suddenly—a storm and hail. We sat and waited, freezing in the cold.

Then we started to work: We struck up the tents, removed the stones, set up the wall around the camp and the barracks. Meanwhile, two more groups had arrived, consisting of 800 men each. Around 9 o'clock in the morning we were 2,000 strong on this mountain. While we were finishing with the ceremony of planting the trees, everybody sounded off mightily with the strains of "Hatikvah."

Suddenly there appeared a British officer and the aide of the district governor. They surveyed what we had done and then said that they were "very sorry" that the weather was so bad (British humor). Then they left. When we had finished with the work, most of us left also. Those of us who remained on the mountain to wait for the orders of higher functionaries numbered 150 haverim. We prepared the camp for the night and got ready to go to sleep. Suddenly there appeared tanks, armored vehicles, and armed soldiers. The district governor's aide informed us that we must leave this place, which we had occupied in an illegal way. Should we refuse to leave, physical force would be used against us. We refused and heard again that familiar refrain: "Very sorry." We were surrounded. Into the circle formed around us rushed British soldiers and policemen armed with clubs and shields (as in the days of King David!). We squatted down on the ground in one pile, each one of us holding another's hand, and started singing "Hatikvah."

The soldiers "went to work." Four soldiers to a man. One would use his club with all he had in him till the man being tackled would stand up. Those that would not stand on their feet were dragged to the trucks. It is difficult to describe the wild sadism of the soldiers—they were for all the world like Nazis, like wild animals, foaming at the mouth. Those among us who speak English let the soldiers know what they thought of them and got for it, of course, particularly rough treatment.

The "battle" lasted all of two hours. The British suffered no casualties. We had two men slightly wounded. The soldiers tore up the tents, demolished the barracks, and dragged us to their trucks. All the way we sang and shouted: "We will climb up to Birya a third time." As we were being dragged away, a new group of 400 men arrived at the ruined camp and, singing, started to build anew. We were taken to Tiberias and set free. But on the morrow, Jews of the old Yishub came with food from Tiberias and Safed. One thousand men and women again set up the camp at Birya. The military again surrounded it, and not till Saturday did they leave. The government gave its permission for the settlement of the Yishub at Birya. . . .

With best regards,
L. Y.

This unique letter, written in 1943 by Captain Joseph H. Freedman, Jewish chaplain of Waterbury, Connecticut, was received by Rabbi Philip S. Bernstein. Captain Freedman and his men, American Jewish servicemen stationed in the Middle East, were deeply inspired by the land of their forefathers. Captain Freedman's description of the religious service held there is a moving one—a prelude to the depth of inspiration and dedication that countless homeless Jews were later to find in this same land.

PALESTINE
1943

DEAR PHIL:

I want to tell you about a recent service that I had conducted that was as thrilling for me as it was for the men who were present. I was crossing the wilderness of Sinai, together with a group of men. It had been a very hot day, as it was during the khamsin, the east wind that blows from the Arabian desert into Egypt and Palestine. The men who were traveling were doing so under the most uncomfortable circumstances imaginable. With noses stuffed with sand and lips parched with thirst, we made camp in the midst of all the barrenness. We had trudged all day over the dry sand, with the sun beating mercilessly down upon us. And as we did so, we thought of our father Moses and the Israelites that followed him over the same way that we were going. Forty years it had taken them, and while it was taking us a considerably shorter time, all of us could not fail to be impressed with the contrast between the two journeys. Undoubtedly both of us, the Egyptian-Jewish slaves, and the American-Jewish soldiers, were bent on the same mission, seeking freedom against those whom we were and are fighting. And yet there was a difference: Our ancestors were slaves, poorly trained and totally unequipped; our men were free men, representing the very flower of American manhood.

There, in the middle of the desert, we camped, and the words of Bamidbar came to me, "And the word of the Lord came unto Moses in the Wilderness of Sinai." Here we were, Jewish boys from Brooklyn, from Philadelphia, from Chicago, from Los Angeles, here we were in the very same wilderness, on the very same sand, inhaling the very same dust, chafing under the very same sun. And I thought: How does history repeat itself! We camped there at the eventide, and from the distance we could see the range of mountains, hard and solid rock, jutting out against the sky. With bated breath, we beheld Mount Sinai in all its glory, just as the sun was descending in its deepest vermilion hue that is so typically Egyptian. Probably our ancestors saw the same deep color, and in it saw the "glory of the Lord descending on the mountain." As soon as the Jewish men realized that we were in the shadow of Mount Sinai itself, there was no constraining them until they had joined in divine worship on the very spot where the Ten Commandments were hewn by the breath of God. Although it was only a weekday and no man was reciting the Kaddish, they insisted on going up the steep rocks so that they could write home that they had ascended Sinai and had "davened" there. And so, just as the sun set, we stood there, a group of Jewish soldiers from America, intoning the traditional words of the afternoon and evening service. And as we stood there, we came upon the words in the JWB Prayer Book for Jews in the Armed Forces:

In His wrath He smote all the first-born of Egypt,
And brought out His people Israel thence to everlasting
freedom.

The words took on an added significance that will always
mean more to these Jewish men than they ever meant
before. The service was ended. I recited the traditional
blessing over the men, and they intoned the final amen.
And as we ended, the sun had already set, a cool breeze was
dispelling the khamsin, and three stars, clear-cut and dia-
mondlike, could be seen in the dark-blue sky. The men felt
at peace, and in the inner recesses of their beings, they had
gained self-satisfaction.

With best wishes,
JOE FREEDMAN

*Sergeant Nathan Sacks, an American serviceman stationed
in the Middle East, wrote the following letter in 1943 to
friends in America. It is unique for the vivid picture it
offers of Jerusalem and Haifa at that time, and Sergeant
Sacks expresses admiration for the dedication and productivity shown in the Israeli collective settlements. It was
the beauty and fertility of these small communities that,
beginning in 1948, would gradually become the nation's
most conspicuous features.*

1943

DEAR R.,

We spent our first day giving Tel Aviv the once-over—
exploring the main avenues, swimming at the beach, a
dance at the Red Cross Club, and a bit of shopping. Americans are still rare, so we rated more than a casual glance by
the local populace.

After our day of orientation, we took a three-day bus
tour, beginning with a trip over the mountains to Jerusalem and Bethlehem. En route we saw beautiful valleys
that were suggestive of some places in the States. We passed
several camps for captured soldiers, fifth columnists, etc.
German captives objected to Jewish guards (for some unknown reason), so they were replaced by Polish guards.
. . . Within a week they begged that the Jewish guards be
turned.

We returned to Jerusalem for dinner and spent the
evening there. An American dentist, in collaboration with
the American consul, had a party for us at which they

served, among other things, good old-fashioned apple pie. There were lots of lovely girls there, and we all regretted that we had to leave Jerusalem the next day.

New Jerusalem is very attractive—buildings are of stone quarried from the nearby hills; everything is clean and orderly; shops are of the type you would find on Fifth Avenue (on a smaller scale, of course). The lobby of the King David Hotel is really very impressive; nightclubs are on the American style—and a heck of a lot better than what we see in Egypt. The blackout is really black—they mean business over here.

Then Old Jerusalem. The Wailing Wall is accessible from only one side and then by climbing hundreds of steps. A few mourners were there, but the day I was there was not a "big" day. The other side of the wall is Arab property and is verboten. You need a strong stomach to go through Old Jerusalem.

That afternoon we left for Haifa, passing a number of collectives and much reclaimed land. The hills and roads are like roller-coaster courses at Coney, and evidently our bus driver was trained on one, for when he came to a hairpin or S turn, he stepped on the gas, and we expected any minute to take off. Guardrails are unheard of. Outside Haifa we stopped at a collective called Shaar Haamakin—a new settlement of Polish and Slavic refugees. Everything was immaculate and modern. They served us cows' milk (for the first time since December, 1942), grapes, and bread with honey—everything from the farm. These collectives are self-sufficient; they even make their own shoes and clothing and grind their own feed, besides schooling their children in the nurseries. Food is scientifically prepared and served to them in the nursery also. We at home could learn a lot from these people—they are doing a job.

The cleanliness of all Palestine impressed us. If I should get more leave, I hope to spend some time there again. Next time no more ruins.

NATHAN

Mrs. Matilda Greenberg, who with her husband and four children moved to Israel in 1933, wrote the following letter to relatives in America. It is dated March, 1948. Although well aware of the threat of destruction and unsure of her family's safety, Mrs. Greenberg expresses the one thing that remains constant and unchanged in the Israeli character— hope, the kind of hope that becomes a reality through concrete plans, hard work, and fervent drives for funds.

TEL AVIV
March 14, 1948

DEAR R.,

. . . Here things are not very happy as you must know from the papers, and this time it is really a very serious time we are passing through. Everyone and everything are affected—and danger lurks everywhere. Business—as you can imagine—is not very flourishing, and the constant acts of violence, repressions, and general insecurity make it feel like camping in the middle of a battlefield while a battle is going on. Every night the thunder of bombardments and firing from the border areas of Tel Aviv–Jaffa keeps one wondering who is doing the shooting, and whichever side it is, there are usually casualties on our side, too. One is constantly paying condolence calls, and the worst of it all is the question "What next?" However, as against this—the spirit of the people is strong and belief in the victory for our cause unshaken.

Every day one sees ground broken for new buildings and projects planned for the future. The youth, in uniform, are serious but gay and they have no doubts at all about the future. It is just such a pity that such spirit must be wasted on the field of battle.

We have endless drives for money—we are now having one for 2½ million pounds ($10 million) for defense, one for a half million for Youth Aliyah, besides for refugees and other smaller drives. There is a lot of work to be done, and all the women are doing some volunteer job or other—with babies, in hospitals, for the soldiers, etc. The older people, of course, are impatient and keep asking "when." Let us hope that peace will come soon. . . .

Affectionately,

MATILDA

In a letter written just prior to the war of independence, David Biderman, a kibbutz member, describes the daily tension and the necessity to be constantly on the alert. The threat of an Arab attack was a twenty-four-hour-a-day threat, and it was the courage among those Israeli youths that later in 1948 would result in the independence of Israel. Mr. Biderman also writes about the difficulties encountered in traveling in Palestine.

KFAR BLUM
January, 1948

DEAR B. L.,

. . . A small notice appears on the bulletin board of the dining hall and states, "There will be an assembly at 9 o'clock. Attendance is compulsory." Before the hour the dining hall is crammed with haverim, some sitting on benches or on the floor, and many standing. Everyone is present—the youth with us for training, the volunteers from the cities, and a few visitors. The chairman of the Security Committee calls the haverim to attention and begins to read out names. There is a dead silence in the room, contrasting sharply with our normally noisy meetings. Everyone's name is read—everyone is given his position. The chairman announces that the kibbutz gong will now be used only for an alarm. The gong outside the dining hall, which was formerly used to summon us to meetings, special functions, lectures, and other activities in the kibbutz, now has only one purpose—to sound the alarm and send haverim hurrying to their positions. The bands of murderers are gathering in our area, and we must be ready. The change in the purpose of the gong is symbolic of the change in our lives. Outwardly, everything is calm and normal.

Haverim proceed with their tasks daily. Inwardly, there is a certain quiet tension, combined with a feeling that everyone knows his place and will be there when the gong rings. . . .

. . . It's about 8:30 in the evening. Supper is still being served in the dining hall for latecomers who have just put their children to sleep. Haverim are in their rooms talking, reading, or listening to the radio. In the distance—so it seems—we hear some rifleshots, but no one pays any attention. Suddenly, the gong begins to sound. We blow out our lamps, the electricity power in the kibbutz is turned off, and everything is plunged into pitch-darkness. We rush outside. Haverim are running from all directions. Someone calls out, "Look out," and we run. I enter a building and sit down on the floor. A number of haverim are there. It is too dark to see who your neighbor is. Someone comes in with a flashlight and summons six of us. We are told, "You go to gate number one, you go to gate number two," etc. These are the entrances to the inner section of the camp, which contains the children's houses. We proceed to our posts and lie down on the ground, waiting. Nothing is heard. It seems like the quiet before the storm. I lie there for a long time. Finally, someone approaches and informs me that I can leave the post. Everything is over. I feel a little relieved and surprised. Nothing happened. Later we learn that one of our neighbors had been fired upon, but that everything is all right. . . . The lights go on, and a crowd gathers in the dining hall. Haverim continue to eat their suppers from which they were torn away by the gong. Others are just standing around. There is a warm and good feeling in the room. It will be okay.

. . . It is 4 o'clock in the afternoon, and haverim are beginning to come in from work to the dining hall for 4 o'clock tea. Today is Thursday—the day which sees our bus bring home the haverim who are working outside the kibbutz. A small group of haverot and children gather around the spot where the bus is unloaded and the passengers get off. Suddenly, shots are heard from the distance, and the firing grows more intense. The convoy is being attacked as it passes the Arab village of Naame. In a few minutes one of our trucks is speeding through the gate with a group of haverim on board. They head in the direction of the firing. Now a large crowd has gathered around the office building, from whose roof the bus and trucks in the convoy can be seen. The shooting continues a little while longer and then ceases. The guard on the roof announces that the convoy is proceeding on its way.

Finally, the trucks and bus come into sight as they turn on the road toward the kibbutz. As the bus drives through our gate, we let out a tremendous cheer. No one hurt. No bus has ever received such a reception as this one. Grinning haverim get off the bus, and everyone eagerly crowds around to get the details. Motke, the driver of the first truck, tells us that the Arab band had placed two roadblocks. Motke never stopped for the first one but drove over it. The engine, fender, and wheels were somewhat damaged, but the truck still runs. He managed to drive around the second one. What were a couple of roadblocks to Motke who had driven a truck through the Sahara in the Jewish units for three years. Ach, these bands, they don't know how to lay a good roadblock. Our supernumerary police tell us they fired quite heavily on the ambushers who could not be seen from the road. We get around haverim who were in the bus. "What did you do, Harry?" someone asks. "I didn't do anything. I lay down on the floor and continued the discussion I was having with my neighbor." Everyone troops into the dining hall. The feeling is the convoys will run and will continue to get through. . . .

The situation has also affected our Arab neighbors as well. . . . The economic life in the Arab villages has been upset by the change of atmosphere in the area. The center of Arab economic activity—trade and barter—is the Halsa marketplace. Arabs from the entire area bring their produce to Halsa to sell and trade in the market. On Tuesday, market day, the roads are just covered with white head-dresses as the Arabs all head for Halsa. On a hike to Kfar Giladi one Tuesday around Yom Kippur, we met this stream of humanity. Imagine camels strutting down a paved highway! Today the Halsa marketplace is deserted. Arabs don't gather anymore. Sometime ago a rumor was spread that Jews had planted a mine in the Halsa marketplace. Hundreds fled in panic, leaving everything behind. Then the Arab thieves who had started the rumor cleaned up and did a good day's work robbing their brothers. There are other symptoms of the present situation. The Arabs seem to be shooting all the time—more frequently at night. The Arabs now have a night watch of their own, and they seem to shoot at every shadow and sound. Their supply of bullets is plentiful, and in addition, the government has distributed rifles in the Arab villages so they can defend themselves against attack. . . . The biggest event in our area was the attack on Kfar Szold from Syria. The shooting was terrific and lasted from 7 to 11 A.M. The haverim did a good job of defending the place. The British arrived after two hours and did a commendable piece of work in cleaning up the band. This proves how relatively easy it would be for them to restore order—if London wanted order instead of chaos. *Davar* carried a cartoon showing Bevin reading the

Tanach, in the Book of Genesis where it states "there was chaos and desolation," and he comments, "Hmm, that's interesting. I wonder how *He* did it." Whatever methods He used, He restored order from chaos, and Bevin's policy is to create the reverse. . . .

You may have the impression that Jews do not travel very much these days since the transport is frequently attacked, mines are laid in the roads, etc. Well, the other week I traveled to Givat Brenner. From Kfar Blum to Rosh Pina to Tiberias we traveled in an armored bus that was filled with passengers and "chaperons." The bus is entirely steel, enclosed with little sliding shutters, which are closed in case of shooting. There isn't much room as the seats have been arranged in a square with a row in the center. There are two drivers—real heroes of Palestine. . . . One was reading a mystery story which was a translation from some U.S. pulp magazine. There appears to be quite a market for this sort of literature. When the driver was through reading, he passed the magazine on to one of our "chaperons" who was sitting up front, anxiously waiting for it. He was a young sabra, about eighteen, and you would never guess from his conduct what a vital job he had. He promptly deposited his weapon on the floor and began to read eagerly. From your newspapers you will know that our area is quite an active one. Convoys have been frequently attacked. The first lap of our journey took us through a number of Arab villages which have been the bases of operations of Arab bands. The trip to Rosh Pina was uneventful, and after a while you stopped craning your neck to look through the small opening overhead. The countryside is hilly, rocky, and ominous, offering excellent opportunities for ambush. At Rosh Pina, a crowd of young people got on and really livened up the bus with their songs. One song was "Swing, Swing, That's the Motto." It was a very swingy tune, so I assume it is one of the latest hits from the United States. They also sang songs of the Haganah which we all know. At Tiberias we changed from our armored bus to a regular one. The trip itself was very interesting, if you forget all the events along the roads. To travel along Lake Kinneret and see the countryside is really an experience. This is Jewish territory. Every few minutes you reach another settlement. Everything is just green. We passed through Afula and Hadera, and everywhere there were lots of people at the bus station. Women boarded the bus with their packages and shopping bags—as if everything were normal. A special Haganah leaflet warns people not to travel unless they must and not to look for the safe seat in the bus. No one knows where it is. . . . When I got on at Tiberias, there was only one seat left, and an elderly man beckoned me to sit down beside him. He offered me the seat near the window—the desirable one in normal times. Apparently he thought he had a "safe" place. As you approach each town, there is a roadblock. The bus stops, and a young fellow jumps aboard and scans the faces of the passengers. At last, I have found the one place where it is an advantage to have a Jewish nose and face—traveling in a bus in Palestine. Yemenite Jews have been complaining that they are being molested by Mishmar Ha'am [defense force] who frequently mistake them for Arabs. Some have written to the newspapers, asking that Yemenites be stationed at the roadblocks so that one Yemenite Jew can recognize another, something which no Ashkenazi can do.

As you proceed along the road, you notice something else at regular intervals—young fellows sitting behind sandbag positions with weapons in hand. Then you feel a little better—the transportation is being taken care of even if you are not aware of everything that is done. We finally got to Tel Aviv from where busload after busload of people was leaving. The buses have changed routes. They travel in convoys, but they move about the country. To Givat Brenner we traveled along a side road because again the area was getting "hot." The trip lasted ten hours, and I was more than relieved to arrive at my destination. I thought of our general secretary and treasurer and the other haverim who travel weekly to Tel Aviv and Haifa—our unsung heroes. . . .

With best regards,
DAVID

A member of the Israeli army wrote this letter in November, 1948, to relatives in America. Besides describing in detail the clothes and regulations of the army, this soldier attributes Israeli's strength and independence—so recently won—to its army. Certainly this new nation's roots were deeply bound in its armed forces—but time would later show, in 1956 and then in 1967, that in actuality the roots lay in each Israeli heart, whether man or woman, civilian or soldier.

November, 1948

Dear T.,

To a newcomer, such as I, the most striking thing about the Zva Haganah L'Israel is that it is a fully organized and modern force consisting of an army, navy, and air force, with sections ranging from general staff to MP's and PX's.

For most soldiers of the Zva Haganah, army life begins in a reception center not unlike the one in which I started my career in the American army. After the traditional processing, the new soldier receives his paybook and uniform. Of course, you realize that when the army was started, barely six months ago, there was no such thing as a uniform; recruits were simply given a list of things that they should bring along.

But now most Israeli soldiers wear the standard design khaki shirts with epaulets and shorts or long pants, depending on the season. The newly designed hat with the short caps in back is similar to that worn by the French Foreign Legion and is very effective in the strong sun which dominates the sky most of the year. Of course, this is Israel, and there are many exceptions to the rule.

You can see soldiers wearing anything from the Anzac cowboy-type hat to the much valued kaffiyeh, the flowing Arab headgear. The latter is particularly popular among the Palmach. The kaffiyeh is worn as a sash around the waist. The proud possessor of such an article of booty usually has a story to tell about how the prize fell into his hands and will usually tell it without undue urging. The sight of a pistol or shiny commando knife hanging from the belt of an Israeli soldier as he dances in a Tel Aviv café is not uncommon. It seems that the current fad of displaying weapons in public is to a great extent a reaction against the days when the mere carrying of a firearm was punishable by death. During the days of the active war, hardly a soldier was seen anywhere without some firearm. But today the authorities have clamped down to a great extent on such practice. However, it seems likely that the whole problem will solve itself when the novelty of having an official army of our own will wear off.

Now, as for the officers: the Israeli army has them as every army must. Even in the old underground days of the Haganah, there were officers—but then no one wore uniforms or insignia of any kind. Now there are insignia for all ranks of noncommissioned officers and commissioned officers up to the rank equivalent to colonel. There are no generals in the Zva Haganah L'Israel. Most men wear insignia on duty, though until recently there has been little of this in the cities during off-duty hours; now insignia are becoming a much more common sight than at first.

A new set of regulations which formalizes many army rules has recently gone into effect. Enlisted men and officers eat the same food but now have separate mess halls. Officers and enlisted men wear the same uniform made of the same quality material. The new pay scale ranges from about $10 to $20 per month. This isn't very much; but cigarette and chocolate rations are given to every soldier, and services such as free laundry and haircuts help out. Soldiers also get free meals and hotel accommodations when they go to town on leave. Still, the Israeli soldier has to be pretty frugal to make his money last until the first of the month.

The new rule which has caused the greatest fuss is the one concerning saluting all ranks above sergeant. Many have argued that it wasn't in the spirit of the Jewish army to salute any man. Also, the saluting of sergeants is a surprising innovation. But the salute is finally here as it is in every army, and it seems to be here to stay.

The Israeli soldier spends his leisure time, when he gets any, in much the same way as do other soldiers. There is the canteena or PX, where he can buy gazoz (soda) or candy and can read the daily papers. In the canteena you can usually find every one of the numerous papers printed in the country, including those in foreign languages, ranging from Russian to English. Woe to the education officer who fails to get the favorite party organ of one of his men. Chess and checkers are popular, and there is some card playing; but I have yet to see or hear of dice shooting in this army. Most posts have lectures and the Israeli equivalent of USO shows regularly. And then, of course, there are movies, to which admission costs about seven cents. At a recent visit to the post cinema I saw *One Hundred Men and a Girl,* with Deanna Durbin, who was still quite young at that time; of course, there were Hebrew subtitles.

The food in the Israeli army is kosher. In every kitchen, pots are painted with big red letters to let any careless cook know which ones are for meat and which are for dairy. Every kitchen also has its mashgiach, who acts as guardian over the kashrut of the unit.

During Succoth every unit builds a traditional succah next to the mess hall, and the more religious men eat there. The lulav and esrog are standard army issues to all units.

But in general, it seems that Orthodox religion is not practiced to any great extent. The attitude of a former member of the Jewish Brigade is typical. He used to go to synagogue regularly in North Africa and Italy so that he could be together with the other Jewish soldiers and the local Jewish community; but in the Jewish army he doesn't have to go out of his way to be among Jews, so the formal part of religion takes a back seat. Still, the synagogues of the Israeli army were as packed on Rosh Hashana and Yom Kippur as in any Jewish community in the world.

The full story of the military effectiveness of the young Zva Haganah L'Israel in its fight against the combined forces of six Arab states is yet to be told in full. But it is obvious, even to a newcomer, that it is the Zva Haganah L'Israel which has forged the state of Israel and given it a place among the nations of the world. . . .

Regards,

F.

*Covering the period of five years, from 1942 to 1947, this
entertaining letter takes the form of a diary. Written by an
American who moved to Israel, it gives a fresh picture of
life on a kibbutz and describes the kinds of responsibilities
assigned to each member. The letter also conveys the thrill
of watching hard work result in a more productive and
beautiful land.*

Winter, 1947

DEAR H. T.,

Finally, I have reached the goal of years of work in the
movement, of hahshara, of talking, reading, preaching, and
hearing—Palestine, Palestine, Palestine . . . the streets,
full of people. Now, at last, I'm here. It is strange, this
realization that all these people are Jews, my brethren—the
bus drivers, the postmen, the storekeepers—Jews, all Jews.
And at last, the kibbutz—the expression of Socialist Zionist
longings, bronzed, sturdy haverim, fellow idealists, my comrades. . . .

Of course, in America, some things are done better. In
America, for instance, the buses run on time. And there is
always room to sit down. Here, things are funny, sometimes
even annoying. If you get a flat tire, the driver shouts,
"Everybody out, and three strong boys to lend a hand." You
sit side by side with a basket of live chickens, bushels of
vegetables, and an oxygen bottle. The bus driver smokes
incessantly and chats with an old pal, seemingly never
watching the road. . . .

In America we have such food— Oh, those steaks, and ice-
cream sundaes. Here in the kibbutz, things get monotonous
—in the tomato season, tomatoes, fresh, boiled, fried,

ketchup, juice, soup; and later, eggplants, made in forty-six different ways and still tasting like eggplant—and there is tea without sugar. And the language is hellishly hard to learn. Nobody pays any attention to me, meetings are over my head, the newspaper is impossible, the news on the radio, nonunderstandable—I wonder what's going on in Palestine.

How gullible these people are! They won't believe that New York has a 100-story building because they get sick when they go up 2 stories in an elevator. So I tell them that for such sensitive people there are buildings with stationary elevators, and the building goes up and down. . . . And they refused to realize that in America most families have automobiles and radios.

It's difficult to realize that I've been here for six months already. Soon I'll be a member, and then maybe I'll be assigned to a permanent place to work. Where? I wouldn't mind working in the vegetable garden, except that I can't stand the fellow in charge. And driving a tractor means working all sorts of hours. Maybe in the machine shop? But can I visualize working years and years at that sort of trade? Anyway, it's easier to get along now that I can understand the language and express myself a bit—but what am I going to do when my supply of English novels runs out? I can't enjoy reading Hebrew. And, of course, they won't devote even a measly ten cents to purchase some English reading material. . . .

. . . My second anniversay in the kibbutz. The place is beginning to look like something—there are young trees and lawns. If only we could manage a few good long-term loans, so that we might buy some new equipment. I wonder who is going to be the next treasurer. Moshe would be good, but he isn't well, and Reuven is too free with money. And Yaakov, well somehow he just doesn't fit into that job. . . .

I ought to do something to fix up the room a bit, maybe make a new easy chair or something. I wonder if Dov would give me a hand—especially since I'll probably be sent out on avodat hutz again soon. Still, I enjoyed those six months in Kfar Giladi—meeting new people, earning money for the kibbutz—but it is fine to come back home. Also, I haven't done a thing since I was put on the housing committee—we need more accommodations and furniture, we'll have to fight for a bigger budget, and there are far too many visitors. . . .

. . . Three years in the place, and all's well. Being editor of the paper was an easy job compared to the work I'm doing now. This business of arranging the daily workboard, of arguing with each and every department head, of allocating the insufficiency of people, of forcing haverim to do a day in the kitchen—as if I were responsible for Batya being sick or that Rivka is on annual leave.

. . . All right, so I'm a veteran now. But I've only been here five years. Does that mean that these newcomers, these halutzim, greenhorns from America, have the right to call me "old guard"? What a funny lot they are—what extreme clothes they wear! After all, I'm not a prude, but there is a limit to the amount of clothes one may take off. These halters, hmmmmm. . . . And their constant use of English is revolting. Don't they know that Hebrew is the language of the country? And now they want *English books,* of all things—let them read Hebrew. Soon they'll be expecting us to turn off the Hebrew broadcasts, so that they can listen to the English news. . . .

And they don't like our food. They should have been here when we couldn't get enough tomatoes. And what is wrong with a succulent piece of eggplant, especially when it's made to taste like chopped herring? We, if I remember correctly, were much more reasonable than these people. What is the movement coming to? Oh, well, another meeting tonight—we've got to discuss the potato fields, and one of these Yankees has some crackbrained idea about a newfangled machine, a potato digger or something. . . .

Regards to all,

T.

In 1949 a Canadian businessman, Bernard Bloomfield, made an extensive trip through Israel. He wrote many interesting and detailed letters to his wife, two of which appear here. In these letters, written from Haifa during the spring of 1949, Mr. Bloomfield covers a wide range of topics, including the excitement of Israel's first Independence Day parade and the extent of its armed forces, the high price and shortage of food, and the somewhat less than desirable hotel situation in Israel during that period.

HAIFI
Thursday, March 31, 1949

DEAREST,

Hotel breakfasts follow a certain pattern. They have no menus, but give you fruit juice, one egg done as you wish, a large dish of hors d'oeuvres consisting of sardines, cream cheese and another kind, marinated herring, coffee or tea, jam, bread or toast. They serve butter, although it is very expensive and difficult to obtain. Most people use domestic margarine, which I found very good. I can't quite tell the difference.

The bread has the same shape as our kümmel loaf but is dark brown and of very good quality and taste. They eat a lot of bread here. There are shortages in many things, including foodstuffs. The country has to import a great deal of what it eats, like grain and meat. Meat is expensive and hard to get. The hotels are given some sort of preference in view of their having to cater to visitors. Generally, one has to queue up and take one's chances. J. S.'s secretary told me she had to pay 80 cents for 100 grams of meat (454 grams to a pound) she'd bought yesterday. Fowl is also very expensive and scarce. Eggs are all stamped, and on the roads leading into the cities, there are check posts which stop all cars and search for eggs or whatever food may be in short supply. The government wants no trafficking in foods on the black market. By stopping people from visiting outlying points to obtain food supplies other than those available in the cities, hoarding and black-market dealings are prevented.

We were surprised once when a conversation took place between our driver and a soldier at a checkpoint. I asked what was going on.

"Looking for eggs," said the driver.

If supplies are in the car, a proper receipt must be shown for them. The government stands for no nonsense when it comes to black-marketeering. We heard of a prominent merchant who was caught, summarily tried, fined some tremendous sum like 10,000 Israeli pounds and sentenced to jail for three years. They had him with his proverbial diaper quite off and gave him the treatment he deserved. Before the sentence was to start, said merchant popped off with a heart attack and saved the state some board and lodging.

I read in the Palestine *Post* where a man was fined 100 Israeli pounds for charging 3 mills more than the controlled price for a kippered herring! Three mills is less than a cent! And so, by really clamping down on the chiselers, they are controlling the black market—for no mercy is shown and no quarter is given.

I observed to Louis how much more effective this sort of action is, compared to what we see at home. There when someone is caught overcharging or black-marketeering, in most cases, when tried, he is given an easy fine and let off with a reprimand not to do it again. He pays up, looks repentant, and scuttles off to see how quickly he can make up the fine again by his same activities, plus a little extra! There is a way to stop this sort of thing, by hitting down with a clap of thunder—as they do here.

The food shops are not like ours. Things are not handled so sanitarily as one would wish or as they do at home. For instance, I saw a butcher shop with a few carcasses hanging in front all covered with flies. Nearby another fellow was selling fish, which were displayed in a box on the street. He would occasionally wave off the flies that gathered thick on them. Then he would sprinkle the fish with water, to keep them fresh. He had a little scale, and he did a thriving business. The shops that sell food have much of it exposed, such as barrels of olives, dried fish, dates, bread. They use no screen doors or windows, and naturally flies are everywhere. In one restaurant we visited there were so many flies hovering over our plates, we got up and left in disgust. If fly screens are ever used in the Near East, the Jews will be the first to use them. But naturally such refinements must come gradually. The Israelis are as vigorous as we in their business methods. Once they return to normal living, things like these will quickly change, and modern markets and groceterias will make an early appearance.

Many of the people in business are not the types we are used to either. They come from all over the lot—Germany, France, Poland, Rumania, Greece, Bulgaria—from every spot in Europe, and they bring with them the habits and cultures of the countries in which they lived. There is bound to be a conglomeration until things get more settled and a sort of uniformity takes hold of their lives.

We went to the quarantine health department and were passed by the doctor, a friendly man who came from Germany. We saw our hunchbacked pal again, and he gave us a cheery and friendly smile. Then to the tourist bureau, where Mr. Sar-Shalom had an itinerary ready for us.

I thanked him courteously. He smiled with pleasure and assured us he was completely at our disposal and to call him if we experienced any difficulty. We then had a cup of Turkish coffee and learned that he had changed his name from whatever it formerly was to Sar-Shalom, which means giver of peace.

Then to J. S.'s office and to lunch. He took us to a restaurant called Pross, and a very appetizing lunch we had, too, considering the difficulties they must have obtaining supplies.

After leaving J. S., we went to pick up some films we had developed. My camera is no good, and I swapped it for one equally as bad. They are very short of film and photo supplies in general. The snaps will be a nice memento of our trip, even if they're not very good.

We took a bus home—we are getting more economical, as taxis are really too expensive. The streets in Haifa are all up and down hill and very tiring. At night, to see the houses row upon row up the mountainside, with their lights glowing, is like a fairy picture, it is so beautiful.

Today we were supposed to leave Haifa and go to the Sharon Hotel in Herzlia. It is perhaps the finest in Israel, twenty minutes out of Tel Aviv, but as we are going to see Abba Hushi tomorrow morning, we postponed it and will take the trip later.

Hotels in Israel are not exactly as we know them. As I said, they are classified into five types. Each class is governed by a controlled rate and gives accommodation, food, and service accordingly. Most of them are very small and contain maybe from three or four to fifteen or twenty rooms at the most. They include breakfast with the cost of the room.

The first price, however, is no indication of the final amount—there are, "plus pluses" as they are called: 10 percent for service—something for the porter—the bus service, and so on. Naturally when the final account is rendered, it is much higher.

. . . To get back to Israeli hotels—there are so few rooms available and so many visitors clamoring for them that it is a troublesome thing to get accommodation when one needs it. This makes travel very difficult. It is essential that more hotels, larger hotels, be built quickly, and in this field lie great opportunities for investment by people who understand the hotel business as it is run in Canada and the States.

In Jerusalem there is the King David Hotel—a fine, imposing stone building. This is the largest hotel in Israel, with about 250 rooms. They had just finished fixing it up after the famous explosion which practically blew up one wing, and it should soon be open for business again.

The clerks in the hotels are an interesting lot. They look at you speculatively and scrutinize you as if to say, "Now why should I give these fellows a room—why them and not someone else?" It isn't that they are looking for extra tips (although who doesn't like an extra tip!), it is just that they feel they don't want to give rooms to people unless they are temperamentally agreeable. We, being always polite and understanding, were very fortunate wherever we stayed. We always went off feeling as though we'd made some more good friends.

. . . The cost of living here is very high. Some prices are quite crazy. Gasoline costs 80 cents a gallon; the cheapest-looking shoes cost around $12 a pair, and so on, all along the line. A common day laborer doing construction work gets around 3 to 3½ Israeli pounds per day. Everywhere are men and women in uniform, soldiers and sailors. They do not have standardized uniforms but wear tunics and pants of different khaki shades. But they do their work, and the miracle of what happened here is something unexplainable.

The British figured that within ten days after they left on May 15, they would be back again in control. But they are through here. Their prestige has sunk very low, as no one (including the Arabs) has any use or much respect left for them.

Today, as we were walking along the street, we saw a truck in front of some military building unloading steel-strapped wooden boxes labeled AID TO ISRAEL, MONTREAL, CANADA. I was on this committee, and it was a great thrill to me, for those were the very boxes we had helped prepare in Montreal.

I fully realize now what the canned food and other supplies mean over here, seeing that a can of green beans or sauerkraut or peas costs here, in the store, about 55 cents.

. . . The harbor is a fine one and shows great promise. With the somewhat antiquated equipment now in use, they are able to handle daily 3,000 tons of incoming cargo and 2,000 tons of outgoing cargo, a very high figure when one considers the equipment is not what it should be. A section of the harbor is marked off as dangerous. This is the area where the S.S. *Patria,* S.S. *Chaim Arlosoroff,* and S.S. *Ocean Vigour* were sunk during the days of "illegal immigration." Parts of their superstructures protrude from the water, causing a serious menace to shipping. They expect to break them up soon and remove the debris.

Many who perished on these ships were unrecognizable and could not be identified when their bodies were recovered. They were given a special funeral and were buried as B'nai Abraham (Sons of Abraham) for the men, and

B'noth Sarah (Daughters of Sarah) for the women. Poor souls. They'd got only a peek at the Promised Land.

. . . We decided to take a bus to Nahariya and pay Amos and Kulli a surprise visit. On the way (it takes an hour by bus) we passed many settlements and kibbutzim, where the traces of battle still remain.

The development of these communal settlements dates back to the first wave of immigration in 1882 and the succeeding ones starting in 1904 and in 1919–23. The immigrants, having had to start from scratch and with little or no resources, realized that communal endeavor was necessary if they were to accomplish anything.

Land was (and still is) provided them by the Jewish National Fund (Keren Kayemeth) on hereditary lease, at a low rental of 1 percent to 2 percent of the value of the land per annum. Most of the capital required for the establishment of the settlements—for buildings, livestock, and equipment—was provided (and still is) by the Palestine Foundation Fund (Keren Hayesod) in the form of long-term loans at a low rate of interest of from 2 percent to 4 percent.

From this evolved various types of settlements, differing in social organization and methods of work. The most common of these are:

Kvutza—a collective agricultural settlement in which land, buildings, and all basic property are owned jointly. The economic principle is that of one large family.

Kibbutz—a collective farm in which the economy is based on industry, as well as agriculture. Members of the group share a common treasury and draw from it in accordance with their needs.

Moshav—a smallholder's settlement in which families

have individual homes and land but operate cooperatively in working their fields, purchasing, and marketing.

Before reaching Acre, we saw one Arab village that had been completely demolished, all except the mosque, which the Jews never touch. The Jews were scrupulous in respecting holy places, no matter whose they were. It is sometimes eerie to see an Arab village or town completely wrecked—not one stone standing on another—but to find the mosque and minaret intact.

All along the road one sees army encampments and, at strategic spots, roadblocks. The boys and girls in uniform are many and are a serious and earnest lot, joking and smiling easily, but with a sort of self-reliance and thoughtfulness. The sights we saw made the war seem very real, even though it is officially over.

Before the war the city of Acre had between 15,000 and 20,000 Arabs. Now only about 3,000 remain. The houses they vacated did very nicely for the new Jewish settlers, as housing is a serious problem here, with 1,000 people a day entering the country. While we were on the docks this morning, in Haifa, we hoped to see a ship arrive with immigrants, but none came. Yesterday 1,800 people arrived. Jacob says it is a terrific sight and so moving it makes him cry every time he sees it.

On the way to Nahariya, one sees kibbutzim on each side of the road. The fields are flat and the earth fertile, and there are irrigation pipes much in evidence, for water is very scarce in many places. Many people from Haifa go to Nahariya for holidays on account of the good air and the bathing, and the water there is said (by the inhabitants of Nahariya) to be the best in Israel.

Just before we came to Nahariya, Louis noticed a factory on the side of the road with a sign PRI MESHEK [fruit of the land] in Hebrew and English letters. We stopped the bus and got off. It was Amos' factory. It is very nice, and I took a snap of it. We surprised Amos at his work. He was dressed like a tank commander in a pair of blue denim coveralls, big rubber boots, and a small wool toque jauntily stuck on the top of his head.

He showed us around the factory. They had been canning sauerkraut and were cleaning up after the day's work. Tomorrow they will can plum jam. They had also just completed a batch of marmalade, which we tasted with great approval. It was excellent and had a nice tanginess to it. Evidently they know how to make a good product.

Their production is about sixty to seventy-five cases per day. Amos says they will increase this, as they are getting some new and improved equipment. I gave Amos an idea for a simple labeling machine I had once seen in a factory and which was most ingenious. It can be made for a few dollars, if they can make it, instead of having to buy one for $1,600. I hope they will be able to follow my description! Amos introduced us to his three partners. We then left for Nahariya, which is about a mile from the factory.

. . . After dinner, we bid good-bye to the family and walked with Amos and Kulli (his wife) to the bus terminal. We stopped at a little open cart on the roadway and bought some chocolate and halvah and then awaited the arrival of the bus. At the station there is a big sign listing all the hotels and boardinghouses, with a space after each name where a little sliding panel can be moved to show the word "Vacancies" or "Filled." An excellent idea that lets people know immediately where rooms are available. We were told a story about one of the women who has a boardinghouse there. Four weeks ago she married an "American" sea captain, who moved in, bedded himself down very comfortably, and commenced putting on weight, enjoying the wonderful food. The marital bliss came to an abrupt end when the lady accidentally discovered that her husband was a Polish cook. She got rid of him pronto.

On the way back to Haifa in the bus—it gets dark very early here—the stars shone so brightly and seemed so close that I was fascinated by their brilliance. I thought of the millions of eyes through the centuries, long forgotten, that had also gazed at them with wonder and curiosity. I thought of the scenes, the stories, and the history that had made this little land the cradle of the human imagination. The mystery and the miracle of all the recent happenings seemed to gather suddenly and blend with the past, and I felt as though I were driving along destiny's road. For here again, after 2,000 long and suffering years, the Jews had come home to their old and hallowed land. The Great Dipper pointed upside down from the way it looks back home. Cassiopeia was all askew from the way I've always seen it, and so were all the other constellations. And then, as we suddenly came to an open spot on the road, along the Mediterranean, the wide curve of the shore showed the lights of Haifa across the bay—all glowing and twinkling up and down the Carmel, and the new moon, like a clean, thin sickle of white cold light, hung in the cloudless dark-blue sky, low and very clear. . . .

B.

HAIFA
Wednesday, May 4, 1949

DEAREST,
Today is Israel's first birthday. One year ago the state was founded. In Tel Aviv there is to be a great parade,

followed by a garden party at Government House, given by Ben-Gurion. . . .

We picked up another couple and set off for Tel Aviv. It was a beautiful clear morning, and the air was fresh and sweet as we drove along—the sea on our right. Arriving in Tel Aviv, we called on Avram and his son, Horky (real name Johannes Hyrcanus after one of the Maccabees). . . . Then we left to watch the parade.

I tried to get Baruch and Dinah Marcus on the phone to tell them we'd meet them at the garden party, but the stores were closed on account of the parade—and believe it or not, I could not find a telephone in Tel Aviv! Incidentally, the telephone system is the same which was in use when the British were here. It is hopelessly inadequate.

The traffic is so heavy that to call Haifa from Tel Aviv after 9 A.M., one must wait from three to five hours. If it is an emergency call, special provision is made and a priority given, but it must be really urgent. It is quicker to make the trip by car.

When I think of the interminable time it takes to make a long-distance phone call, send a cable, or buy stamps, I realize how far advanced we are at home where quick service in such things is quite taken for granted. Here one cannot send a cable over the phone. It must be taken to the cable office. One can buy stamps only in the post office— nowhere else. I once stood in line thirty minutes to get airmail stamps for a letter to Nery. And when I finally came to the wicket, the girl told me she could not change my pound note—there is a silver shortage here. Some merciful soul came to my assistance, or I'd still be standing in that line!

The streets were now jampacked with people all along in the direction of Allenby Road, up which the parade was to pass. We found a good vantage point in the apartment of an acquaintance, overlooking the street. We saw echelons of Spitfires flying in perfect formation across the city, swooping over the rooftops in exhibition flying. There were Flying Fortresses, too, and I felt goose pimples at the perfect handling of the planes as they went through their paces. That the Israeli flyers gave a good account of themselves in the war is plain to see!

Finally, the parade came along. There were tank squadrons, universal carriers, antiaircraft batteries with mobile searchlights, light artillery. Camel corps units marched picturesquely by, and the medical corps, with donkeys carrying stretchers and first-aid equipment; walkie-talkie units—even carrier pigeons in the cages mounted on trucks—and as always the good old infantry. It was an eye-opener to see the scope of the services and equipment that had made the Israeli forces a compact victorious army. The spirit and military bearing of the soldiers, sailors, and airmen were magnificent and would do credit to any country in the world.

We arrived at the garden party in the Kirya rather late, as we were held up by traffic. Just as we were going in, Baruch and Dinah were coming out to meet us, as previously arranged. The affair was held in the open. It was attended by the members of the Knesset and their wives and friends. All the foreign diplomats and military attachés were there. A band played nicely, and refreshments were served. The Prime Minister and his wife were hosts. Baruch introduced us to some of the members of the Cabinet. We met Golda Meyerson, who remembered us from her visit to Montreal last year. . . . We met David Remez, minister of communications, a sincere and capable man; Eliezer Kaplan, minister of finance; Moshe Shapiro, minister of immigration. . . . But all the while, I kept asking Baruch, "Where is Ben-Gurion? I want to meet him!"

Just then we came upon the Prime Minister and were formally introduced to him by Chaim Halpern, director general of agriculture. Baruch spoke to Ben-Gurion first in Hebrew. I don't know what he said, but Ben-Gurion turned to us and engaged in friendly conversation. He asked us what we thought of Israel, and we gave him our enthusiastic reply. I told him I had listened to his radio speech the night before, when he talked to the nation about the dangers of inflation. I said that although I did not understand Hebrew, I enjoyed his speech.

"What part did you like best?" he asked me.

"The part where you thumped the table and said, 'Profits are too high; prices must come down.' "

He grinned and seemed pleased. Then, turning to Louis, he asked, "How many people will you send us from Canada? We like Canadians and want them to come here."

Louis thought for a moment and said, "We'll give you fifty thousand in the next ten years."

Ben-Gurion laughed and said, animatedly, "I can't wait ten years; we need them now!"

Then the band played "Hatikvah," and I got a real thrill as I saw everyone stand stiffly at attention for the national anthem, the foreign diplomats and attachés included. It was an experience for them, too—many of them good and loyal friends—to participate in Israel's first birthday ceremony. The whole world is watching it grow with interest. The baby is a lusty one!

B.

1950's

THE YEARS OF GROWTH

For Israel and her people the 1950's were years of growth and years of problems. During this decade following her independence and following the productive years of the 1940's, it appeared as though the fruits of her labor would yield too little nourishment. The overwhelming number of immigrants converging on that small area threatened to burst the boundaries of Israel's limited agricultural and industrial productivity. Dishearteningly, a woman who had lived in Israel since 1933 wrote, ". . . whatever we have must be divided among so many more people, and so there is not enough for anyone."

However, it was not just the inadequacy of Israel's resources that created problems. The hundreds of thousands who came to settle in Israel after World War II were survivors of a dreaded persecution and war. Their immediate memories were wrapped in their losses and suffering. They were desolate and homeless—a different kind of settler from those Palestinian Jews who had lived on and known this land for centuries or those who had traveled to Israel and made her their homeland by choice. Yet these immigrants brought to Israel a new and poignant loyalty. At one time having had everything taken from them, they cherished even more possessively the security of having a land of their own.

For a while the hardships and shortages were felt everywhere. A kibbutz member wrote that life meant "less food, less housing . . . a cut that takes weeks and weeks to heal because the food you are getting doesn't have enough of that something it should have . . . one pair of shoes a year and maybe a coat."

As an adolescent might express a confusion of ambitions, so at times Israel's efforts in self-improvement were somewhat overzealous and impetuous. One example was her extensive reforestation programs. An American living in Israel wrote, ". . . there is one sad fact about the tree planting; there is a tendency for trees to be planted with much ceremony and then quietly neglected to their death in the following month." But on another level a purpose was still served. Not only were those trees planted for their beauty, but they also provided work for hundreds of unskilled laborers, and so one of the benefits lay in reducing unemployment in the young nation.

Then, in 1956, Israel once again prepared for war. A member of a kibbutz observed, "It's amazing the security precautions taken here and how fast and efficiently we mobilized. Within twenty-four hours we were completely prepared for anything."

As had happened in the late 1940's and would happen in 1967, the crisis created a labor shortage in an already fragile economy. But the Israeli civilians—the women, children, and the elderly—united to relieve many of the nation's pressing responsibilities.

Thus, the years of growth did not mean years of successes. But growth in maturity often occurs through errors, and Israel's experiences as she expanded and developed, agriculturally and industrially, served only to double her efforts. By now her successes and failures added up to an investment in the land that could only be expressed by the deepest love. Time would prove that a vigorous and creative adult was being formed during those years of growth. And despite the difficulties and doubts of the 1950's, there was quietly emerging a force whose power would finally be known in June, 1967.

A former member of a kibbutz writes, in 1951, about his conflicting feelings concerning Israel. The shortage of food, clothing, and public utilities and the confusion created by the influx of immigrants from so many different cultures add up to, in this author's mind, a perplexity of feelings not easily expressed in words. But as confusing as that adolescent nation's growing pains were following the war of independence in 1948, the Israelis' hopes and labors never wavered in their goal for a better and more secure future.

JERUSALEM
April 4, 1951

DEAR W. P.,

. . . You can get initiated to Israel only by coming here to live. The Israel you get to know outside the country is one which filters through many persons and institutions. And filtered water and filtered light and filtered Israel are not like the unfiltered—and less pure and less comprehensible, perhaps. I know what you mean by the silence that seems to take hold of people once they arrive in the country. I daresay, not to excuse it, that you will have much the same experience when you finally arrive.

For example, 100,000 Iraqis and Rumanians in the next four months can become a wonderful propaganda slogan or an ideal example of what Zionism means today in these times of kibbutz galuyot. These are relatively "pure," filtered conceptions. To live kibbutz galuyot, as revolutionary as it really is, means also to get used to it, to become accustomed to it and to all its subtle, all-penetrating, all-enveloping implications. To the ordinary person, it means less food, less housing, longer lines here and there, black markets, a cut that takes weeks and weeks to heal because the food you are getting doesn't have enough of that something it should have, one pair of shoes a year, and maybe a coat, a Babel of languages and confusion of faces, customs, demands, costumes, aspirations, literacy, public hygiene, and so on and so on. Each one of us has to live his own segment of life here and elsewhere, and each one of us gets his own very incomplete and often distorted picture of what is happening around him. Centuries separate men and the Yemenite woman who sits next to me on the crowded bus. The nearly twenty centuries are more than time. She is the product of an entirely different world. We barely understand each other. But now add to her and to me, all the others of us who have come and are still coming. How can I tell you about her and all the others when I sometimes doubt whether I can understand what is happening to me and what I'm living through? We are, all of us, very small people living through unbelievable days and creating, sometimes against our wills, this thing called Israel. Who knows what it is or can understand it? One thing is becoming clear: We are the generation of the wilderness that must die off before Israel in the larger sense can be created and shaped. Each one of us remembers the pots of flesh in our own personal Egypt. We can't help remembering Egypt and acting as if we were once in Egypt. We are human and have all the human qualities, even here.

Having to read the Tanach for my studies, I have come to love it in a way which is impossible in the Galut. And not only to love as much as to understand. One of the deeper and more personal experiences here for me has been to read, for example, some of the parts of Bamidbar. When you came here, you will for the first time feel and understand how present it is. A stiff-necked people who are being led and sometimes forced to their Promised Land in spite of themselves. I recall sitting in the bus (the location of much education) one night, on my way home from work, and an argument broke out between a young fellow and a couple in back of him, and the young fellow said, "We had more meat when the British were here. It's better they were back in place of our government . . . !" This can be repeated over and over again by substituting for meat things like job, house, etc., etc. What truth is there to "reveal"? Perhaps the "truth" is love, love for our people (and not necessarily for kibbutz or kvutza or party) . The test of love and love itself, in practice, must be experienced to be understood, and it must be lived. . . .

My best to all,
B. T.

In a letter written in September, 1951, Mrs. Matilda Green-berg describes some of the adverse conditions experienced by inhabitants of Israel during those difficult formative years. Although she complains of trying to run a home under trying conditions, it was these very problems that provided her, along with countless others who held a deep faith in Israel, with a source of inspiration for and dedication to a better future.

TEL AVIV
September, 1951

DEAR FAMILY,

. . . I suppose there is no need writing you about us—Israel is well publicized. Naturally the everyday life of the people is not news, and all you get in the newspapers are some versions by this or that visitor, and so on. From all of them you may perhaps be able to piece together a sort of picture of what goes on. So far we're still going, and, every day almost there are a thousand more of us who come in from all ends of the world, and this, of course, is one of our great difficulties—whatever we have must be divided among so many more people, and so there is not enough for anyone.

Just this minute I had to stop—a case in point—because the increased demand for electricity has put a strain on the existing plant (new generators take a long time to get; they are ordered but may take a year or two). So the use of electricity is curtailed, and it is entirely undependable. I just had to light a candle and am now writing by candle-light. I can't use my electric stove when I need it—the hours that are allowed are very inconvenient, and then sometimes it is shut off even during the hours when one is permitted to use it. I, for the first time in my life, have started to use a kerosene wick stove (one burner) —and so we are conditioned, and that, I think, is all right.

Today I was out shopping for the holiday. I got one pound of carp for the three of us and one pound of meat. Of course, I don't want you to feel sorry for us, as we are among the lucky ones who have family and friends in the United States. I already have some chicken and meat which I bought with food checks we received from the folks and some friends in Chicago—but I am just trying to give you a picture of the conditions here. Yet in spite of it all, people are gay and joke about all our problems, and life is not at all dull. All of us have better figures now—Max lost 45 pounds and looks much better and feels better. I now weigh 125 pounds, which is about 10 to 15 pounds less than I weighed before, and I, too, can say that I feel fine. I guess it's a sign that people eat too much.

When we go around the country with tourists and see that vast developments are taking place and the still great need for development, when we see the myriads of immigrant camps, the sense of values changes, and some of the things we considered so important lose some of their urgency. (The lights just came on again!)

For one thing, we cannot fall into a rut here. There is always something to be excited about—both good and not so good—but it keeps one on his toes. I personally am quite busy, what with being a grandmother with two grandchildren and some extracurricular activities like the Junior Hadassah Children's Village and the Society for Crippled Children, which is now building a new clinic, and I am busy helping in the planning of the buildings and program. . . .

Love from all of us,
MATILDA

Mary Clawson, an American living in Israel with her husband, Marion, and children, during the 1950's wrote many fascinating and enlightening letters to friends and relatives in America. In the following letters Mrs. Clawson writes warmly and informatively on a variety of subjects. She describes in detail her visit to the Israeli parliament, the Knesset; she gives a humorous account of her encounter with a Jerusalem policeman; she tells of her delight with the language of the Israelis; and she describes the rewards and frustrations of the many Israeli reforestation programs.

JERUSALEM
November 12, 1953

DEAR MARGARET AND HERMAN,

. . . I visited the Knesset, Israel's parliament, the other day. It does not seem very much like our Congress, except for the general hustle and bustle and the feeling an outsider gets that here is the center of government. The most memorable characteristic of the Israeli government, from the Prime Minister to the messengers, is its informality, an informality which is combined with dignity. This trait reaches into many aspects of the government: In summer, few men, including Cabinet ministers, wear neckties; high and low officials have coffee or tea together in the same cafeteria; no official I have heard of finds it beneath his dignity to stop and chat in the most friendly way with all kinds of people. In what other country can one find a famous Prime Minister, such as David Ben-Gurion was to Israel, resigning in order to tend sheep in a settlement in the Negev, where he and his wife do all the regular work of other members and do it in the desolate, barren, pioneer atmosphere of Sdeh Boker? In Israel this is not a particularly astonishing phenomenon. I cannot imagine its happening anywhere else in the Middle East or anywhere else in the world, for that matter.

There is only one house of 120 members, including, at present, 9 women and 8 Arabs, representing fifteen political parties. Mapai, which is more or less moderate Socialist, is the largest party. There are three religious parties, ranging from moderate religious labor to rabid Orthodox. The Herut Party is interesting, if far from admirable from my point of view. Herut members have strong Western learnings; they are chauvinistic in the extreme, and the symbol of their party depicts the map of Israel including Trans-Jordan.

The Knesset building is not impressive; it is a converted block of flats and banks in the center of Jerusalem. The building is attractively arranged; but it is too small, and there is too little space around it. The Knesset has been meeting here since January, 1950. The first meeting was in Jerusalem in February, 1949, in the head office of the Jewish Agency building; later it was transferred to Tel Aviv and then back to Jerusalem. The government is constructing a new and impressive-looking Knesset building not far from where we live in Beit Hakerem, but, like some other projects in Israel, work on it is sporadic because of lack of funds.

We had a personally conducted tour; the result was we understood a lot more about what we were seeing than we would have otherwise. Just as you enter, you see an immense menorah (seven-armed candelabrum), given by B'nai B'rith of Brazil, on a stair landing. It is quite handsome but needs more space around it. The conference rooms look very much like conference rooms in the Department of

Labor in Washington, not the most elegant ones, either, and they are not as spacious or as well furnished as most of the conference rooms I saw in the Department of the Interior; they cannot compare with similar ones in Congress. There was a judicial committee meeting going on, with men in open-necked shirts sitting around a table drinking juice or coffee and talking in a serious fashion; there was also a religious committee meeting, where all the members whom I could see wore the traditional black skullcap of the Orthodox, which, to my non-Jewish eyes, looked odd in a parliament working room. Oddest of all, however, was the sight of a white kaffiyeh on the head of someone who looked very much at home in one of the office rooms. I had forgotten that there are Arab members of the Knesset.

There is a good-looking library of between 15,000 and 20,000 volumes in a variety of languages, headed by a man who came from Hebrew University (and aided by a staff of assistants) . These people serve the members of the Knesset. There is also a reading room with all kinds of periodicals and a lending library. It is not the Library of Congress, of course, but handsome nonetheless.

We got seats in the first row of the visitors' gallery, where we could look down on the floor and hear the debate. Members are seated in rising circular tiers facing the Speaker, who is flanked on one side by the clerk of the Knesset and on the other by the rostrum from which members address the house. Slightly to the rear of the Speaker, there are seats for the deputy speakers. Members of the largest party sit on the left of the Speaker and then go around the floor in accordance with the size of their party's representation. There is a glass compartment near the Speaker where an interpreter translates into Arabic for the Arab members, who have earphones attached to their desks.

As we were listening, a member was speaking fairly heatedly, giving what he was careful to say were his personal opinions on the Religious Judges Bill, then before the house. He was saying that it was his belief that those who fill the posts of rabbis should not be rabbinical judges. Some woman member kept interrupting him to air her views on the discriminatory laws against women perpetuated by the bill; I thought it not to her own interest to interrupt the speaker, since, after all, he was opposing the bill, too. But it made the proceedings more interesting for the spectators. In a short time the speaker was told his time was up. There is no filibustering in the Knesset. For major debates the time for the discussion of each bill is decided by the house committee, and parties get speaking time in proportion to their sizes. They then submit the names of the speakers who will take up the time allocated to each of them.

The Knesset follows the British practice of a government's (which is chosen by the leader of the largest party) accepting the responsibility of forming a Cabinet and continuing to operate so long as the government has the confidence of the house. But the President charges the party leader with forming a government. It also follows the British procedure by which the initiative in the matter of legislation is taken by the government, which submits its bills to the house for a first reading or discussion. The Religious Judges Bill, which was being debated as I visited the Knesset, was in this stage. Once a week members may submit questions to Cabinet ministers and move debates on any topic they wish. Votes are then taken, and if the majority wishes debate on a certain topic, it will be held.

The house sits for about eight months of the year, three days a week. There is a summer recess of two months in September and October, designed to cover the period of the

High Holy Days; then there is a month's recess at Passover time and a week each at Hanukkah and Purim.

In addition to the general informality, I was impressed by the large number of spectators in the visitors' gallery. It was filled to overflowing, and we only got front-row seats through some sleight of hand performed by the official showing us around. He told us the gallery is more often than not just as full as the day we were there. Anyone can get tickets of admission by applying a few hours ahead of time at a Knesset office opening onto the street. . . .

Regards,
MARY

JERUSALEM
November 20, 1953

DEAR GAIL,
. . . You should have seen me the other day holding forth on Zion Square, the center of downtown Jerusalem. To get a driver's license in this blessed town, you have to know all the international motor-vehicle signals, and you are supposed to know a great deal about the mechanics of a car; but though I have had a license for three or more months, no one has ever shown me the rules for driving around Jerusalem. I suppose, as at home, ignorance of the law is no excuse, and I should get hold of them somewhere; but so far I have not done it. Anyway, the other day I parked on a street right in the center of Zion Square for a few moments while I went into a shop, and then I left and drove away on various errands and was gone for an hour or more. I parked again, at exactly the same spot, where, in my

innocence, I had arranged to pick up some neighbors. They were not around, so I went into a café to get some coffee; I had not been in the café more than two minutes when one of the neighbors came dashing in after me, announcing that a policeman was giving me a ticket for parking over half an hour in Zion Square. I was justly outraged, tore out and told the policeman, with a neighbor as an interpreter, as he spoke no English, that I had been there only two minutes. He insisted he had seen the same car there an hour ago and calmly went on writing out the ticket, whereupon I became indignant. I screamed; I yelled; I stamped my foot, to the joy of the gathering crowd in Zion Square, declaring that I had been there only two minutes, that I had a witness who would swear, if necessary, I had been in her house in Rehavia ten minutes earlier. The poor policeman had beautiful large brown eyes with a soulful expression; he was most handsome, mounted on a white horse, and began to look alarmed.

Such a crowd collected that a police inspector came up to investigate, and the neighbor had to tell him what it was all about. I was such a picture of outraged innocence that the police decided to call it all off and tore up the half-written ticket. The soulful-eyed policeman told my neighbor to tell me that I should not talk that way, and he imagined that I would not talk that way to a policeman in my own country. He was wrong; I would, if it cost me $50. Also, he asked her for her name and address so she could be witness that he had been polite to me in case I sued him. She, the devil, told him to pay no attention to me, that I was a very nice person, but I came from Mexico, and all Mexicans are excitable. That, he understood, I guess, because to my astonishment he bowed and rode away.

I had no idea what got into him and didn't know until we were well on our way home. Another neighbor and I giggled for some time; the interpreter and prevaricator was still too harassed to think it funny. I have since found out that one is not supposed to park on Zion Square for even a minute; I do not know what he meant about my being there over half an hour. Every time I pass a policeman now, I scrunch down in the car seat and hope to goodness I am being law-abiding and that I look properly respectful.

I thank my lucky stars almost every day that my States license was still valid when we came to Jerusalem, so I did not have to pass such a test in this city. I would never in the wide world pass such a test. I know, because one of my neighbors tried to get a driver's license not so long ago, and I rode in the back of the car while the examiner rode in front with her. She has driven at least 100,000 miles in New York, passed both the international-signals and mechanical test 100 percent, but was flunked cold on the driving test. She is an excellent driver, is calm, has poise and self-confidence, and is quick on the uptake. If I had not been in the back of the car and seen how she drove, I would have thought that for some reason she went to pieces for the examination, but she did not. According to the examiner she was flunked, among other reasons, because she had too much self-confidence for a beginner (she isn't a beginner, of course) ; she did not wait long enough for the pedestrians at a busy intersection (she waited a full two minutes; guess next time she should wait two hours, because in Jerusalem, pedestrians never pay any attention to cars) ; and she did not give a "poor donkey" (I quote) enough room. . . .

Regards,
M.

DEAR DOROTHEA AND PAUL,

. . . Ever since the Zionist era began, Jews all over the world have sent money to plant trees in Palestine or Israel. Part of this region was forested a long, long time ago, but the forests were gradually destroyed. Some of them were cut to make charcoal for fuel; the same thing is going on in Mexico today. It broke my heart to watch it when I was there. Some of the forests were destroyed by goats that ate seedlings right down into the ground. There were also various other causes. Reforestation of Israel is something dear to the hearts of Jews. There are all kinds of stories in the books we read to the boys about "planting trees in the homeland."

Reforestation has also provided a type of public work for the unskilled unemployed ; the money spent on it has been governed as much by the need to relieve unemployment as to plant trees. Carobs, whose pods yield animal food, two types of pines, some cedars, and other conifers are the most common kinds of trees to plant, although eucalyptus has also been quite widely used, especially along the highways. As a native northern Californian I love the eucalyptus; if there is anything more fragrant than the smell of eucalyptus in the rain, I do not know it. These types of trees have only limited commercial value, but Marion says he has been told no better species are well adapted to Israel's climate. A lot of money is spent on tree planting; in some places, for instance, along roads, the trees are watered during the first summer so they will have time to get their roots deep enough to survive. This kind of care is, however, expensive.

Usually trees are planted with an accompaniment of

speeches, music, and parades, especially of schoolchildren, and forests are planted in honor of someone, mostly war heroes, American Zionists, victims of the Nazis, or prominent non-Jewish statesmen.

Some handsome forests are growing up; in the relatively short time we have been here, we have noticed the difference along the road from Jerusalem to Tel Aviv; the hills look more tree-covered than when we came. But there is one sad fact about the tree planting; there is a tendency for trees to be planted with much ceremony and then quietly neglected to their death in the following month. This is not true everywhere, but there is too much of it. There has been some of that even in our shikun. On Tu b'Shvat we planted many trees in our garden with much joy and celebration. Since then some of them have died from lack of water. Marion cannot bear it, so he has taken it upon himself to water them regularly.

One man wrote the Jerusalem *Post* recently, saying it was understandable that the youth who planted a tree in January would want to cut it down, dead or alive, in September to build a succah, but he did object to the carelessness or worse, by which brush fires were allowed to destroy young trees in the hot summer. Fires have become more common in Israel lately as tree planting has been expanded, and this man was pleading for more care this spring and summer.

Marion says this tree planting and later neglect are characteristic of other aspects of the Israel economy. He claims he sometimes thinks that Israel is like the brilliant adolescent son of a rich father. He knows he is brilliant, because he has seen evidences in his schoolwork. He does not want to get ahead on his father's wealth but wants to make his own money and to achieve other attainments as well, and he knows within himself that he can do it. But at the same time he must have his Cadillac convertible, and he plans one magnificent scheme after another, to none of which he gives sufficient attention and hard work to push through to successful completion. All this time he blithely ignores smaller achievements he might make. I think this judgment may be harsh, but it has enough truth in it to make me laugh, even if I am prejudiced enough to laugh ruefully. . . .

Regards,
MARY

JERUSALEM
December 17, 1953

DEAR GRACE AND JOHN,

. . . Hebrew, which in the past few decades has been raised from the dead, or at least from a vehicle used principally for prayers, is every bit as fascinating as one would expect in such reincarnated language. It is now the mother tongue for sabras my age and younger, though for the many immigrants it is an acquired art, sometimes a precarious art. Three things about Hebrew I find especially captivating: the many expressions in everyday use which take you back 2,000 years; the Yiddish expressions; and the English words, descriptive of objects or events unknown in Biblical times.

When Danny tells a friend apropos of a piece of cake, a book, a ride in the bus, "I like it," what he is saying when translated literally is: "It finds favor in my eyes." An art or handicraft is "work of thought" which came from the time artisans put decoration around the Temple. If you cannot sleep, "sleep is wondering away from you," and if you serve guests, you "honor" guests. A bitter man is a man "who is bitter of soul," and both English and Hebrew use commonly the Biblical expression "stiff-necked." But if I do drive myself to learn Hebrew, it will be largely because of the current songs that are popular, especially with teen-agers. There are four I know of right now, which are sung on all kinds of occasions, and which come directly from the Song of Songs. One Danny sings in his Gan, and I have played the record for over two months in complete ignorance of the words. What Danny sings is: "The voice of my beloved! Behold, he cometh leaping upon the mountains, skipping upon the hills." This is one of the more common kindergarten songs. Three current teen-ager favorites are: "I am black, but comely, O ye daughters of Jerusalem. . . . Look not upon me, because I am black, because the sun hath looked upon me. . . ." Another one begins: "Behold, thou art fair, my love; behold, thou art fair; thou hast doves' eyes." And the last one sung today all over Israel begins: "My beloved is mine, and I am his: he feedeth among the lilies. . . ." These songs are set to beautiful Oriental music and are popular dance tunes.

Then there is the Yiddish, now a part of the modern Hebrew slang. Israelis, and probably Jews in general, find it hard to believe, but neither my husband nor I had ever heard the word "nu" until we came to Israel. Jews are under the impression this word is used internationally; it may be, but it had passed me by, though it is now a Clawson family word. You would find it amusing to hear Danny say, "Nu?" and shrug his shoulders and hold out his hands expressively, because Marion helped him put on some clothes but got sidetracked somewhere with his shoes. It is such an easy way to say, "Well, why don't you hurry?" or "When will we get going?" or "What shall we do next?" The girl who explained the meaning of the word to me told me she has a friend to whom she had not written for months. Finally, a postcard came with only one word on it—"Nu?"—meaning in this case: "What's the matter with you? Why haven't you written me and when are you going to do it?" There is also the Yiddish word "nudnik" which means pest, and maybe it is derived from nu; I guess a pest is someone who keeps asking, "Now what?" The *le* added to the end of words as affection also comes from the Yiddish. Our neighbors were entertained when Patrick started to call me Mommyle. Children here call their parents Abbale or Imale constantly—that is, when they feel kindly toward them or want something they have a suspicion they should not have.

It has been a problem to bring the old Hebrew language sufficiently up to date so it can be used effectively now. A body of experts work on the problem almost constantly, so we are told. And many are the stories about the favorite Israeli pastime—discussion of fine points of Hebrew grammar or discussion of which words are best to use for modern terms. Marion tells me that once in a while a conference on agricultural problems that has been tending to drone along suddenly comes to life, with heated arguments flying back and forth. His assistant, who interprets for him, almost always whispers at this point that the members have started to argue about a fine point of grammar or use of a word.

There is quite a list of English words in constant use in Hebrew; I suspect there are even some sabras, with no English connections, who are unaware of the derivation of these words. Here are just a few: "cocktail party"; "baby-sitter"; "puncture"—this means any kind of a breakdown, whether of a car or a burned roast or cake; "tramp"—which means a ride, such as a ride to Tel Aviv (a "trampist" is perfectly good Hebrew for hitchhiker) ; "television"; "telephone"; "racketta" is a rocket ship. "Primus" is anything that makes life miserable; a general nuisance in other words. This comes from the primus, a kerosene stove which works on pressure, is noisy, hard to keep going, exploding at the slightest provocation; almost any other kind of stove is preferable. I am told that in the kibbutzim any time a third person is put in a room which formerly held two people, he is called a primus. Every once in a while Danny tells me with surprise, "You know, Ima, it is almost the same word in Hebrew that it is in English." There is "sandvich," "svetter" (sweater), "giraffa," and lots more.

It is not a musical language to my ears; it is rather guttural; but I like to hear it spoken, and especially I like to think of the Biblical expressions being used in an everyday sort of way. . . .

Regards,
MARY

*During the fall of 1956 relations between Egypt and Israel
once again deteriorated. Israel prepared herself well during
the Suez Crisis, as revealed in these letters written by an
American member of a kibbutz. Covering the period from
October 30 to November 6, the letters express the heroism
and perseverance of both the Israeli civilians and the armed
forces—qualities of strength that, in 1967, would gain the
attention and respect of the entire world.*

October 30, 1956

Dear B.,

All's well with me and with Israel. We hear that Israel is
advancing on Suez and that we've occupied some Egyptian
outposts. I'm sure Herut (right-wing party) is happy about
this even if America isn't. . . . Everyone goes on with his
work, not worrying, not showing any visible signs of
tension.

Today I again worked sewing beads together for the
children's bunkers. Now we're not so sure that they won't
need them.

The only thing that worries us and makes for most of our
conversation is that we'll be sent back. This is tough to take,
but if we must, we must. I'd feel like a traitor going out
because everyone can be of great help to fill in the jobs in
which all our men, who have been called back into the
army, used to work.

Another blackout tonight, nationwide. All we can do is
sit and pray. Maybe the situation isn't as bad as we make it
out to be. I certainly hope not. Certainly it is hard to take
going back to America . . . without fulfilling our plans.

It's getting so I can't talk or think straight anymore.

Everything changes so fast that by the time the Jerusalem *Post* gets here, the "news isn't news anymore." At any rate, I'm not worried over my skin. . . .

My Hebrew is progressing very slowly as I speak too much English. Half the kibbutz is originally from England and America, you know.

Today at 4 o'clock I'm going to be working in the grounds around Beit Habonim. We're fixing the earth in the expectation that we'll plant trees and flowers. . . . Everyone from the kibbutz asks half-jokingly, "Aren't you gone yet?" Everyone talks of being sent back. Everyone is preoccupied with this unhappy possibility. . . .

October 31

. . . Our army finally asserted itself, and we are winning. We are very happy. The news has come that we have in our possession an Egyptian destroyer. It surrendered to us this morning with 250 sailors, after shelling Haifa all night. We got a lot of artillery on that ship, too.

We had a national blackout last night, and at 1:30 A.M. all the children were herded into the bomb shelters and into the beds we've been sewing for them. Unfortunately some of the beds collapsed and had to be sewn again this morning. We're learning.

Our men, all those who are left in the kibbutz, did guard duty last night. All but 30 men have gone to the reserves. Things are popping, especially rumors. This is very upsetting as we never know what's true and what is not.

This morning a rumor came through that we had orders to leave. We took this very hard. Imagine anyone not wanting to go to America. . . .

Life goes on. We live till the next news broadcast. Happily the Jordanian border was the quietest in the past eight years, claims the Jerusalem *Post*. We taught them a lesson.

The American Embassy is advising us to leave because of the situation. Happily we are not so badly off as the Americans seem to think. I'm sure the events of the past week or so will have a big effect on the elections. We expect that all will clear up in a few days, and we can return to normal.

It's amazing the security precautions taken here and how fast and efficiently we mobilized. Within twenty-four hours we were compltely prepared for anything. Our windows were all pasted with strips of paper to prevent shattering, trenches were cleaned, bomb shelters painted, beds sewn and made, and numerous things were done. Children take care of messages. All night long, kids take turns at the kibbutz's phone taking military calls and relaying messages and information. Only military calls come in at night. . . .

November 2

Yesterday we didn't have Hebrew class, as there is a big labor shortage here. We worked eight hours thinning sugar beets. Blackout as usual and a lecture by Aryeh on the situation in the cities.

Yesterday a destroyer, unaccompanied by other ships and planes, shelled Haifa. Not one single shell hit the beach. They all fell into the water. Israeli ships and planes got the ship to surrender in thirty minutes. It was wholly unprecedented for a ship to give itself up. A fleet, yes. But one ship, no. . . . One ship always sinks, destroys, or sabotages itself so as to prevent the enemy from using it afterward. The paper said that the Egyptians jumped into the water, and some of the 250 captured were in their underwear.

In the morning there were police guarding the piers, but Haifa went to see what we had captured and pushed the Israeli police aside. One guy was so excited that he fell into the water and had to be fished out.

We downed seven MIG's, and this morning hundreds of Egyptian planes were bombed by the British. Gaza gave up today, but what to do with all those Arab refugees . . . ?

The Arabs are scared stiff of us, judging by all their actions in the fighting. You should hear Radio Cairo. It keeps reporting fabulous gains for Egypt and terrible losses for us. Boy, do we laugh!

Altogether 100 people took the three destroyers and four transport planes that were brought in to evacuate the Americans. What a laugh and rebuke to the American government. If so few people went back, you should know that the situation isn't as bad as painted by the papers. . . .

November 6

. . . Well, the physical battle is over. Now we have the political front to face. It will be much more difficult to win.

Every map of Israel will need altering. Minor, but nice.

Our blackout has been lifted, and the men are slowly returning. The kibbutz will soon be back to normal. It got so that we were living from broadcast to broadcast, worried and on edge. Now we are confident that everything will go well.

We're hearing fantastic stories of the fight, tragic, heroic, and comical. For instance, when our soldiers took over

Gaza, the Arabs came out yelling in Hebrew, "Long live the state of Israel."

The Jerusalem *Post* said that our soldiers were complaining because the Arabs refused to fight, and they felt cheated. The Arabs ran out on the positions and deserted. Many are voluntarily surrendering. We hear of fantastic numbers of POW's, anywhere from 5,000 to 20,000. What will we do with them all?

The men who have returned tell us that they almost went crazy with boredom on the front. They would sit and play Scrabble all day and night. They devised a system of tying ropes together to all their legs so that if anything happened while they were asleep, someone would jerk the rope and wake everyone up.

The kibbutz really has suffered these past few days with all its men gone. Some areas of work were closed down completely.

Some boys and girls from the nearby town of Kiryat Shmona have been helping in the beet fields lately. They are from Casablanca. I've never seen such a bunch of dead-end kids in my life; twelve- and thirteen-year-olds smoking and swearing in Arabic. It's good I don't understand the language.

1960's

THE MATURE ISRAEL FACES CRISIS

For the Israelis the 1960's will be remembered for one year—1967. That historic week in June, 1967, was a turning point for their nation. But Israel's victory in the Six-Day War created no turning point in her own eyes; rather, in the eyes of the world she was finally recognized as a vigorous force in world politics and as a fully mature and stable nation.

Her victory amazed the world. Yet the one least amazed was Israel. As always, it was the Israelis themselves who fully recognized the depths and strengths of their devotion to their homeland. It had always been a quiet and restrained strength. It was the same strength that had nourished and supported their labors during the 1940's, which had culminated in their independence. In 1948 and in 1967 each man, woman, and child had known that as individuals their lives were worth the sacrifice for the life of their offspring—Israel. In 1967, as in the 1940's, it was once again the quietness and the serenity of the Israeli's dedication that clashed violently with the hysterical accusations and harassments by her neighbors. Israel's swift and controlled mobilization of her armed forces and civilians formed a national strength and unity far different from the "strength" of the Arabs. Their "strength" had all the characteristics of a chaotic and frenzied stampede.

That week in June was described in one of the following letters as "a miracle and a nightmare." But the real miracle lay in the power and unity of the Israeli civilians. During the period of preparing for combat, one teacher wrote that "even the children are helping—everybody wants to do something." After reading these letters, you will feel that everybody—even the old and the infirm—did something. Those days of crisis were filled not only with preparations for their defense, but also with prayers for the boys and men in combat. Yet the death of any single person was secondary to the fear that it was Israel who might die in battle. The dangers of combat are poignantly expressed in many of the following letters. One woman wrote, "I cannot tell you what a bullet hole looks like over the crib of our only grandchild."

Israel defended herself with great courage. But in a sense that courage was not greater than the courage of her labors during the 1940's to make barren land fertile and to achieve independence. It was a courage no greater than that with which she had faced her many difficulties during her years of growth and development. Israel's courage lies, not in any *single* crisis or in any *one* achievement, but in her daily labors and love for her existence.

*The following letters were written by Harold Greenwald,
a New York attorney who spent the summer of 1967 in
Israel with his wife, Dot. The two letters were written
eight days apart. The first letter describes the intense "calm"
that pervaded the country before the outbreak of war. The
next letter, besides giving the reader a concise résumé of the
events leading up to the war, tells of the self-sacrifice and
courage that characterized the spirit of the entire Israeli
population.*

TEL AVIV
June 5, 1967

DEAR FOLKS,

It is 11:45 A.M. Dot is shopping for staples, plastic water
carriers, blackout paper, etc. I am at the phone, waiting for
some of our friends to call in the news, which has filled the
ether, but in Hebrew. There is news in English—from
Jordan. From it I learn that the war of revenge and annihi-
lation has started, that our brave airmen shot down forty-
four Israeli planes in their gangster raids on our sacred soil.
This is not too discouraging. I had no idea Israel owned
forty-four planes to start with.

These are the facts as we see them. The nation is fully
mobilized: there are few men on the streets; we can see
antiaircraft emplacements, one mounted just a block away
on the Dan. There has never been a calm like this calm.
People are quietly and conscientiously attending their tasks,
some at offices, some in stores, children in school, house-
wives sticking up black paper over their windows, girls
filling sandbags, older men finishing trenches, boys picking
up and delivering mail. The radio from Israeli Jerusalem

interrupts its classical music, from time to time, to broadcast a bulletin or to call out the names of added units for mobilization. Come to think of it, the calm is contagious.

In synagogue this morning we heard the first air-raid alarm sounded. No one lifted his head from the prayer book. The attitude is not at all either one of overconfidence or "Let George do it." There is no room for doubt because there is no alternative. Israel must fight to survive. And she is not willing to have other nationals fight her fight. The best she can hope for, if the past is any guide, is for others, her "friends" included, to stay out of her way and not hinder. In today's amoral international world, realism is synonymous with cynicism.

My attention returns to the noon news. The Hebrew announcer speaks a tongue unhappily foreign to me, but he speaks quietly in measured tones. Our friends across the border also speak a foreign tongue, but they shout, much in the style of Hitler.

My crystal ball remains cloudy, but yesterday's facts do not vanish in today's conflict. Nasser is now a prisoner of his own bombast. Jordan stuck her head into the Egyptian noose with her eyes wide open. Arab unity is superficial and will withstand neither victory nor defeat. And from where we sit, the Arab doom is defeat.

Dot just returned. We have food supplies, water containers, but apparently will have to spend the evenings in the dark. No complaint.

Some of our Israeli friends urge us to leave—they tell us we will hardly make a substantial contribution to their war effort and perhaps impede their's through burdening them with concern. Perhaps they are right, but as we see it now, they will just have to put up with us for the present. This conflict will determine whether they have a country or not. If they do, we mean to share it with them.

Now, is this a way to spend a vacation?

Best to all,
DOT AND HAROLD

TEL AVIV
June 13, 1967

DEAR FOLKS,

What went before is past remembrance. Accordingly, this can hardly be deemed a continuance.

Time stood still as Israel was poised on the brink of disaster, not knowing whether any of the "great" powers would raise a hand and prevent her and her "neighbors" from crashing over the brink. Time has now accelerated its pace—it seems much more than a week since we heard our first air-raid siren. In the interim, the world has been shaken, and Dot and I along with it.

This can hardly be objective. We are much too close to it all. Our proximity is too great, our involvement too immediate, our interests too personal. But it seems that to find a parallel miracle one would have to reread the Bible. (Not a bad idea—for military tacticians, as well as for the rest of us. For Dot and me, particularly, who look forward to visiting the Wailing Wall, the Cave of Machpelah, and the Tomb of Rachel.)

In the city, the tape is being removed from the windows, and shopkeepers are replacing valuables on display. At home, pictures are being rehung, blackout paper is taken down, and the light of this glorious Israeli sun is again filling our hearts. Men in uniform are seen on the streets, a

Uzi gun on one arm, a smiling gal invariably on the other.

Over the past several days, tears flowed—copiously, unashamedly. There was a mingling of grief and pride.

Pride in the armor, which cut the Sinai like the scalpel of a skilled surgeon removing malignancy. Pride in the navy, which entered Port Said and Alexandria and sank missile launchers and subs. Pride in the infantry, which stormed up the eastern banks of the Jordan and the Sea of Galilee to blast bunkers and silence Syrian artillery from which northern settlements were shelled. Pride in the defense forces generally, which completed their assignments cleanly, methodically, and with a minimum of civilian loss.

Last, but not least, pride in a home front, which carried on sustained by faith, although burdened by concern for loved ones, which can stem only from the Jewish concept of the nobility of man and the sanctity of human life.

Yes, the Lord worked a miracle, as in the days of the army of Joshua. On the field of battle, the number of tanks, planes, guns, and forts taken will be counted. An inventory will be compiled of vast quantities of booty. Generals will marvel at the impregnable strongpoints overrun, impossibly difficult topography ignored, invincible odds overcome, vast distances through rough terrain traversed, logistics solved, and war plans conceived and executed. To all these complexities there is but a single answer—a miracle was wrought.

The hand of the Lord was extended over the home front, too. The people were acutely aware of their danger. Dot and I could only guess at and question the degree of its imminence and nature. But our neighbors were no strangers to it. Many of them had faced it several times before. But it was faced by all, calmly, quietly, and confidently—all with an inner glow that defies description and comprehension by the non-Israeli. Patrick O'Donovan, writing for the London *Observer,* summed up his reactions by saying, "It makes one ashamed not to be a Jew." Many Jews outside Israel will reply, "It makes one ashamed not to be an Israeli." There was no less bravery and stamina at home than on the fronts. Israel was surrounded. We knew that on her Independence Day, when we were in Jerusalem. The threats, reiterated too frequently to be ignored, to strangle her and push her into the sea, were about to be put to a test. We knew that, too. As more Arab leaders jumped to support Nasser, there was a good and increasingly better chance that the threats would be carried out. And we knew that, too.

I repeat—that those threats were not realized, that the very contrary was accomplished, is nothing short of a miracle. The miracle can now be the object of rejoicing among our friends, amazement among our "neutrals," and despair by our enemies, but its true dimensions will be appreciated only in the perspective of history.

The instruments through which this miracle was effectuated were, in themselves, miraculous. In the three-week period following Independence Day, the atmosphere was tense. Absent intervention by the States, primarily, Nasser and his cohorts obviously were embarked on a collision course with Israel. There was general recognition that a dictator can advance only, that any retreat is an admission of weakness, and that, therefore, Nasser was becoming increasingly a prisoner of his own haughty mouthings. Had he quit after U Thant's precipitate surrender, he would have been unmistakably the czar of the Arab world. Had he quit after occupying Sharm El Sheikh without closing the Strait of Tiran, he would have been in a dominant bargaining position with Israel. But his closing of the strait and firm statement of refusal even to negotiate made it impossible for him to retreat. And, for Israel, there was no alternative. During that three-week period of waiting for the deadlock to be broken, as was promised but never achieved, Dot and I were swamped by entreaties from most of our friends to leave. We were prepared to do so, but only at the point where our continued presence could have become a real burden to our Israelis. We would not eat their food or drink their water or jeopardize their safety by preempting their air-raid shelters, but we decided that if Israel was determined to ascertain, definitely, at whatever cost, whether or not it was to be a land in which Jews could live, we, Dot and I, were resolved to share that land, if it survived, with them. To say that we are grateful for the decision is to give expression to the obvious.

An advertisement by our ambassador "advised" U.S. citizens not having urgent business in Israel to leave. Dot saw to it that such urgent business was undertaken. I agreed that our drapes needed replacement and that our chairs required new slipcovers. Our Israeli upholsterer assured us that everything would be "besedder"—okay. When Dot commented that she was more concerned about the Arab situation, he reassured her that *everything* would be okay— Israel and the drapes, too. Two days later, he went into the army or, rather, on active duty. Israelis are always in the armed forces, sometimes on home leave or "vacation." Incidentally, some of the drapes have been hung, but our chairs are still in his shop. When they are delivered, perhaps his man will help me remove the sandbags with which our propane gas tanks have been covered.

During those three weeks our senses were really strained. We were aware of intensified activity in the skies. Planes were heard, but evidently flew too high to be visible. Helicopters ran a constant shuttle from the airfield just north of the Hilton Hotel to their destinations somewhere to the south. Air-raid shelters were readied. Trenches were dug, and the sand so excavated was put in bags by the women and carried away by the men, everyone working calmly and in a businesslike manner without the slightest indication that their industry was in any way alien to their normal pursuit. Things had to be done, and things were being done. It was that simple.

A vacant lot across Ben Yehuda Street from our house was dedicated as the site for a new synagogue. The following morning the same people who had joyously participated in the dedication ceremonies, chanting the prayers, singing the songs, reciting the psalms, were again in the area—digging, filling, carrying.

The first air-raid siren sounded in Tel Aviv at or about 8:30 A.M. on Monday, June 5. I was then in synagogue—my father's yahrzeit. This, then, was the opening of Israel's third war for independence. The worshipers looked up from their siddurim, exchanged knowing glances and resumed the shacharith (morning) services. There were six or seven additional air raids that day. Dot and I felt like animated Yo-Yo's—more angry and annoyed than fearful. Shots could be heard—sounds, I thought, of the antiaircraft gun which was mounted on the nearby Dan Hotel. In the shelter, one young girl placed her hand on her sister's head and whispered, "That's just an open door that's slamming." At the time, we were being shelled from Jordan. Their markmanship was bad.

Between air raids, Dot visited the shops and bought, among other staples, cake flour. Those who know her can share my amazement! We're in a shooting, not a political, war, and she's stocking up on cake flour! Not ordinary flour—cake flour! We still have the stuff. I never did get around to using it. Yes, it was not for baking at all. You were told to make a paste of it, soak cloth in the paste, and stick the cloth to the windows. Prevents shattering, or so we were told. Anyhow, it was something to do, but I didn't do it. There was too much radio to listen to—all from Arab stations, all uniformly bad. Most of it sounded plausible—forty-four Israeli planes could have been shot down attempting to bomb Cairo. Egyptian tank brigades could have cut the Negev from Gaza. Jordanian troops could have pierced the narrow neck toward Natanya. Haifa might be cut off. But when they claimed to have occupied Tel Aviv, my presence on our terrace notwithstanding, I was reminded of the drunk in the bar who made one claim too many. Later that day Kol Israel started to broadcast the news, and its broadcasts, although a good deal more acceptable, sounded not a bit less fantastic. You know the facts and figures.

On the streets and in the shelters there was no gloating—just the prayer for a swift and merciful victory and the end of nineteen years of bombast by day and terror by night.

There are stories by the dozen—touching, revealing, tender, inspiring, humbling.

Erich Leinsdorf, heeding our embassy's "advice" took off, leaving Roberta Peters and Richard Tucker behind to continue their concerts and, incidentally, to entertain the troops. We were in the Mann Auditorium that evening and helped Tucker bring down the house, joining him and the Israelis in an emotion-laden "Hatikvah" as ever has been sung. Yes, it was good to be alive and in Israel.

During the period of waiting—waiting principally for our country to implement words of advice and agreement—a delegation of women—not militant, blustering men, but women—whose sons, husbands, and brothers had been mo-

bilized and were sitting out the waiting weeks, picketed
Mapai Party headquarters, around the corner on Hayarkon
Street, and demanded that Moshe Dayan, the hero of Sinai,
be appointed to the Cabinet as minister of defense. Their
demand was based on the view which, by that time, was
generally accepted—Israel would be the beneficiary of advice, and advice only, from her enemies' friends. There was
a job to be done, and to do it, Israel would receive no help.
Get it over with, and call on the man best suited to take the
lead.

I asked the demonstrator carrying the placard (in Hebrew, of course) whether the incident would not be inter-
preted in the foreign press, whose representatives, cameras
in hand, were present, as revealing a split in Israeli politics
and was told, "We're not particularly interested in their
slant. We're tired of waiting while the enemy adds to his
numbers. Our morale is high, but our boys cannot stand
still forever. We've got to fight now, or we'll be strangled."
Surprisingly, one of the cameramen turned to me, nodded,
and said, "She's right." I didn't think so at the time, but
with the benefit of hindsight—I now agree. Dayan's appointment completely relieved the charged atmosphere.
Waiting no longer implied indecision. If Israel waited, she
did so only to be sure. From then on, Israel spoke with a
single voice—the people and their representatives alike.

The shrill cries of Arab radio announcers, not unlike the
hypnotic rantings of Hitler, were in sharp contrast with the
voice of Kol Israel. Even while Arab claims of disastrous
defeats inflicted on Israeli armies were being reported, the
announcer retained his normal, modulated tone. The de-
meanor of the people was just too infectious to be shed.
Under these circumstances, who could even think of
leaving?

It is ironic that those Arab claims, repeatedly broadcast,

hour after hour, were indeed believed. If Nasser knew that Radio Cairo was lying, Hussein did not. And if Jordan believed its own propaganda, Egypt surely did. On Tuesday, the sixth, a flight of eleven Algerian planes, flying to be in on the kill, approached an airport on the Sinai Peninsula and requested permission to land. The tower, in Arabic, invited them in. They landed and were taken over by the Israelis, who had captured the field the previous day.

By Tuesday our shelter had become a community center. The civilian wardens reported on the news of the previous night and early morning. While patrolling the street, they carried portable radios and heard an Israeli pilot, downed near Ismailia thank a helicopter crew who flew in, far behind enemy lines at the time, to rescue him. Quietly and quite matter-of-factly he said, "Nice boys—you came in to get me."

In combat, one Israeli pilot was heard to say, "I've got that plane. He's in my sights . . . I've hit him . . . He's down in flames . . . There's another plane . . . I've got him in my sights . . . No! I'll leave him for my buddy here . . . After all, what's fair is fair."

Last night, Shabbas Eve, we had dinner at the Hilton. The few guests at the hotels are reporters. Two correspondents, both British, sat at adjoining tables. One, eyes bloodshot, had just flown up from Sharm El Sheikh. It had been horribly hot, he said. Among his unpublished news items was one giving the other side of the gruesome air struggle. Another Israeli pilot, who bailed out also at Ismailia, was hacked to pieces by civilians who captured him when his parachute landed. He had been shot at during his descent. The correspondent told of the carnage on Sinai—thousands of Egyptian soldiers, shoeless, wandering over the desert, headed for the Suez Canal. Many, he said, would die of thirst. Many were traveling in circles. Some, attempting to cross the canal, had been shot at by Egyptians on the west bank, who had mistaken them for Israeli invaders. He was, with his fellows, astounded by the speed and scope of the Israeli operations. A large Egyptian tank column, pursued by Israeli tanks, raced into the Mitla Pass in retreat westward. On emerging from the pass, they ran into Israeli armor and were wiped out. He spoke quite freely, and when he learned that we had been in Israel before hostilities began, we exchanged questions and answers. Yes, he had just flown over the canal. There were some ships in it which seemed out of position, but he didn't think the canal was impassable. The Sinai campaign was unequaled in efficiency, skill, daring, and endurance. He saw some of it (was detained with all our correspondents by the Israeli authorities all day Monday), but by the time he was allowed to join the military, they were so deeply engaged in Sinai that the complete rout of the enemy was a joyous conclusion.

We told him that men with whom we had just spoken said they went without sleep for three solid days and nights, living on bread and black coffee, and he remarked, "No wonder the Egyptians were trapped in Mitla."

He spoke in glowing terms of one tank commander, who had been "kind" to him and who, he feared, had been killed in action. The Israeli casualty lists show a high percentage of officers to men. When Ben-Gurion mourned the loss of the flower of Israel's defense forces, he knew whereof he spoke. The Israeli commanders lead their forces. That may be one reason for their astounding success. . . .

Best to all,
DOT AND HAROLD

*This exciting narrative about the Six-Day War was written
by Mrs. Anna Shenkman in a letter to her son Ted. Mrs.
Shenkman vividly describes how she and four others—all in
their seventies—lived together during this crucial period,
drawing the reader into the midst of the hectic activity both
inside and outside the house. Once again it is apparent that
the dedication and selflessness of the civilians matched the
courage and will of the fighting soldiers of Israel.*

JERUSALEM
June 14, 1967

MY DEAR SON TED,

. . . Yes, I know, being Americans residing here in Israel
the past several years, we could have been evacuated along
with our other Americans; but we could not leave your
brother Yigal who was mustered into the Israeli army with
all able-bodied civilians. It was not an easy decision for Dad
and me to make. The Israelis were so calm, so brave—we
could not leave them, and by the grace of God, all of us,
including the Ruppin family, are safe.

There are so many things I want to know—so much I
wanted to tell you. So I've decided to write and, in my
simple way, try to tell you how we lived through the days of
terror here in Jerusalem.

While we, civilians, could not believe the big powers and
world opinion would let the Arabs attack us, we followed
instructions and readied ourselves for whatever emergency
was in store for us. There was no panic, no inflammatory
speeches, no hatred—just a calm resolution to resist and
prevent another destruction of the Jews.

(Interruption—Yigal just dropped in! He had a chance

to visit Gerda and was returning to his post. A car with soldiers was waiting for him downstairs. . . .)

And so we were told to get a week's supply of fresh food and staples for emergency. Most of the people did just that, and there was very little hoarding.

I always cook on Friday for Saturday and Sunday. This Friday, June 2, I cooked even more, hoping to have either Yigal or Gerda or both for the weekend. But they did not come, and the tension was becoming unbearable. By this time it was clear that while the great powers were procrastinating and filibustering, the Egyptians were moving closer and closer to Israeli borders. To demand of Israel to wait much longer was unfair and disastrous, to say the least.

The radio announced Moshe Dayan was appointed minister of defense, and people sighed with relief. Monday morning we heard that the Egyptians crossed Israeli borders in the south, and heavy fighting was raging there. We thought of Yigal and prayed.

At 12 o'clock, when the children were coming home from school, the shooting started here from Jordan. At first it was not too bad. Dad and I, according to instructions, filled up the bathtub and pots and pans with water. Our maid came to clean. She was frightened and nervous, so I told her there would be no cleaning. She would just help us paste tapes over the windows, but we did not have time to finish. She hardly worked twenty minutes when a terrific crash shook the house, and we ran downstairs to Mrs. Ruppin, as was previously arranged.

On the way down we met our milkman, an elderly man. We took the milk and asked him if we should pay him. He shook his head and, with tears in his eyes, said, "If I'll be shot, I won't need the money. If we survive, there will be plenty of time to collect."

In Mr. Ruppin's house there was a feverish rush to black out all the doors and windows with cartons and black paper. Mrs. Comay, the wife of the Israeli ambassador to the UN and now adviser to Abba Eban, came in to help. But as we came down, another blast put the electric lights out, so we worked with candlelight. It was becoming really dangerous to stay close to the windows, so we worked at short intervals between explosions.

Our maid presented a problem. She wanted to get home to her two children and blind mother. It was hard to see her suffer, so Mrs. Comay drove her home and came back again under heavy shelling. This was one of the many brave things women did during these critical days. Every woman with a car volunteered her services, and the needs were many—and urgent.

It took us a whole day to cover up the windows, for there were many of them. Between the heavy shelling, Dad and I brought down our cooked food. Cooking the first three days was out of the question. Twice the electrical power was hit, and our Frigidaires were defrosted. Uncooked food was definitely spoiled.

Mrs. Ruppin's house is well built of solid stone. She has a few rooms in the inner part of the house, not exposed to the street, and she also has a corridor in the middle of the house which has no windows and solid doors leading to three rooms. In this corridor they were sheltered during the siege of Jerusalem in 1948 and survived, and she hoped we would survive again.

Mrs. Ruppin shares her home with her sister and her husband, Mr. Ginosar. . . . So Mrs. Ruppin, the Ginosars, Dad, and I—five people past seventy—in a blacked-out house with food enough to last a week, were prepared to meet our destiny. . . .

The first night we were not alone. Mrs. Ruppin's son came here for a conference and could not return—the roads were blocked. Her brother came in from Haifa to attend a meeting of the Knesset (parliament) where Moshe Dayan was to be sworn in as minister of defense. Her nephew from Tel Aviv was also here on business.

Mr. Ginosar was settled down near the radio. The lights were still on; but the following day they were out again, and we used transistors. The rest of us sat near him, listening to the news and talking quietly, while outside, without stop, thunderous shelling and whistling from planes went on and on. Some blasts came so close and were so powerful it seemed our house was hit, but we were all right. Then a telephone call came from Carmela Yadin, Mrs. Ruppin's daughter. All through the fighting Professor Yadin, her husband, was in Tel Aviv acting as military adviser to Eshkol. Behind the scenes he played an important role in this victory. He had called his wife to tell us not to worry. We are having a colossal success in Gaza and Sinai, and the Egyptians are retreating. So we had this news before it went on the radio, and it braced us up. But the fighting near us was hard, and the casualties were heavy because the Israelis were careful not to damage the ancient shrines in the Old City.

We went to bed—but we didn't sleep a wink.

Tuesday. We were up early in the morning and dashed to the radio for news. We learned we were winning, and all the shelling and shooting we were now hearing was from us to Jordan.

Late in the afternoon Carmela came in for a few minutes. From the start she had mobilized women with cars to offer their services. Since very few buses were operating and some bus lines were closed altogether, these women were helping civilians with transportation in emergency cases. They also picked up hitchhiking soldiers on their way to camps within Jerusalem. They delivered packages of cakes, cigarettes, chocolates, etc. to the different camps, and now, with so many wounded soldiers and civilians, they were collecting sheets and pajamas and delivering them to hospitals. A very difficult job, but Mrs. Yadin is a veteran underground Haganah worker and an excellent organizer. I asked her what women volunteers could do in the hospital. She said, "Nothing." A few women came, but doctors asked them to go home. They were a nuisance running around in corridors, asking the busy, harried doctors and nurses, "What can I do? What can I do?"

After Mrs. Yadin left, a woman doctor from Hadassah dropped in, a friend of the family. She had been on duty a whole night and a whole day and was on her way home for a short rest and back to the hospital. "Yes," she told us, "there were many casualties, many surgery cases. There were plenty of doctors and nurses, but not enough operating rooms. Corridors were full of people on stretchers awaiting their next." And I pray and comfort myself that no news from Yigal is good news.

The doctor then told us of her good luck. She was called to a telephone, and when she returned, the chair she had been sitting on was shot—a bullet in it.

That night, again we did not sleep. I heard rumbling of heavy trucks as some military vehicles went by. I peeped through the window and was faced with such oppressive darkness that I drew back in alarm. As I lay there awake, there suddenly rang in my ears the American national anthem—"Oh, say, can you see. . . ."—and I thought of those brave young Americans who wanted so much to be free, and I prayed that these persecuted, hunted people here should also be given a chance to live in their land of the brave and the free.

By Wednesday morning the shooting had subsided considerably. This was the day for the maid to clean the house; but we knew she would not come, and I knew that unless I did something, I would go mad. I told Mrs. Ruppin the house needed cleaning. She agreed with me, and the two of us pitched in. She cleaned the kitchen and bathrooms, and I vacuumed all the rugs and mopped the floors. My swollen hands, my high blood pressure, my heart—I was not aware of anything. I just kept busy and tried not to think. Not a word from Yigal.

As I was warming up our dinner, I heard Mrs. Ruppin call, "Come, Anna, your Yigal is on the phone!" I ran— Yigal's voice! "Yes, Ma, I'm fine. Are you all right? How's Dad? Sorry to have dragged you into this war. Please call Gerda. Yes, my unit was right here. Just came from the Wailing Wall! What a sight! Can't talk much, Ma—a line of soldiers behind me are anxious to call their folks. . . ."

Later in the afternoon Mrs. Ruppin's brother burst into the house. "I was in the Old City! On Mount Scopus! And by the Wailing Wall! God, it's a miracle! I tell you it's a miracle!"

Tears were brimming in his eyes. He had had a hard time getting a permit to go there, he told us. His son-in-law is a commander of that section. So, after identifying himself properly, he was allowed to go through. He did not want to eat. He did not want to drink. He kept talking and describing all the familiar homes and streets they were not allowed to see for nineteen years! Suddenly he grabbed an apple and ran off—to Haifa, to his wife!

An hour or so later Carmela burst in. "I just came from Mount Scopus!" she exclaimed. "I visited the Wailing

Wall!" And in detail she described the condition of the old Hebrew University, the Hadassah Hospital, the cemetery. Everything that was Jewish was miserably neglected and many places completely destroyed.

How did she manage to get there? As you know, Mount Scopus belongs to Israel, but the Jordanians never permitted access to it. According to the truce agreement in 1948, 120 Israeli soldiers were to be stationed there and relieved by convoy every two weeks. The agreement was observed, but this time the 120 Israeli soldiers were stranded there and shelled. The military knew that Mrs. Yadin was in charge of packages for soldiers. So an officer was sent to her to get the packages. Yes, she had the packages, but who and how would they be distributed? Would she like to accompany the officer? Would she! Just then, Mrs. Comay, who was with her, approached. "Where are you going? To Mount Scopus? Me, too!" And off they went for the greatest moment in their lives.

This Wednesday night we slept a little. It was almost quiet, with only occasional bursts of sniping. Thursday morning I opened the kitchen door and let in the sunshine. The bank and stores were opening up, and Dad went out to get some money and do some shopping. Then I heard some banging—loud and rapid—was it shooting again? I looked through the kitchen door across the backyard—and what do you think I saw? Women, vigorously beating rugs and mattresses that were used in shelters! A few hours later, balconies were decorated with clean wash hung out to dry! This is a sight tourists complain about, but to me it was the most beautiful sight to behold. Israel came back to life!

After lunch, while we were resting, Mrs. Ruppin again cried out, "Look, Anna, here is your Yigal!" And there he was—his face drawn, but sunburned and vigorous, his eyes shining excitedly, and a happy grin on his face! He looked at us searchingly. "Are you all right?" he wanted to know. "Really? I worried about you more than I did about myself. I could have come yesterday but did not want you to see me right after battle. Oh, I have so much to tell you!"

He could not eat—he had just a cup of coffee. He stayed with us less than an hour. "Have you got a clean pair of socks for me? And a windbreaker?" We promised to get what he needed and asked him to return tomorrow for the things. We gave him some cigarettes and chocolates and some brandy, and he left! At once Dad and I went downtown, walking back and forth, for there was still no transportation. We got him the windbreaker and some good woolen socks in a military surplus store.

The following day, Friday, I cooked a chicken dinner. Mrs. Ruppin made delicious knaidlach [matzo balls] and Yigal came—in a hurry—ate his dinner, picked up the things we bought for him, and went off. We did not see him or hear from him until Tuesday evening. His unit had been moved from Jerusalem to Hebron. One fellow, with a car, was going to Tel Aviv to see his family, and Yigal got permission to go with him. He asked his fellow driver to stop by our house just long enough to say hello, and he did the same last night on his way back to his post.

Although the war was over by Thursday, there was still a lot of sniping and mine explosions, and there were and still are daily casualties. Mrs. Ruppin would not let us go until the blackout was officially lifted. That happened Saturday night. Sunday morning, after breakfast, we moved up to our apartment. We were always good friends with Hanna Ruppin, but this week, facing a great danger together, brought us even closer. As I began collecting my pots and pans, Mrs. Ruppin started pushing food for me to take upstairs. I would not have it—so the food was being pushed back and forth until we reached a compromise. We were to have one more meal together and finish all the leftovers. It suited me very well, for our apartment was a mess, with doors and windows open a whole week, with beds unmade, furniture moved away from the windows. There was a lot of cleaning to be done—and still without the maid—and I worked a whole day at it.

Many homes around us were badly hit, and closer to the border, the destruction is great. Our house remained intact. I found a bullet on our stairway and a piece of shrapnel on a sandbag that protected our gas ballon, right by Mrs. Ruppin's kitchen door. A bullet must have hit our water tank on the roof. It was leaking. But that is all. Yes, God was merciful to all of us, and we are grateful, and our hearts go out to our bereaved families here where losses are so great, so heavy, so hard to bear.

It makes my blood boil when some countries tell Israel to be humane toward the Arabs. They were and are and will be humane! For that is the makeup of the people.

You should have heard the Arab leaders on their radio—shrieking with hate. They did not teach their people to be honorable soldiers. They taught them to be bloodthirsty murderers! "Kill," they shouted. "Kill with nails, with teeth!"

You will probably see pictures of armaments in the Sinai Peninsula stretching along the desert, of the latest and most destructive type, missiles, and gas—all directed toward a tiny strip of land with the smallest Jewish population. It was again the miraculous case of David and Goliath—the big bully with a chicken head!

And yet, in spite of all that Israel had to endure, the wounded Arabs are picked up, as well as the Israeli. I have been told of a certain dramatic case of an eleven-year-old Jordanian girl, Hadiya Abu Gardia, who was brought back to life in Sh'arei Zedek Hospital in Jerusalem on Tuesday night after having been pronounced dead. She was found by Captain Nissim Ben Israel with a wound in her neck when Israeli forces entered the Deir Abu Tor quarter across the Jordanian border. Brought to the Jewish hospital, she "died" on the operating table, but the doctors wouldn't give up and used an "ambu" resuscitation machine; the child was brought back to life, and her mother was permitted to visit her in the hospital. And this is not an isolated case, for the doctors are helping all the wounded—Jew and Arab alike. When the Old City was captured, immediately all sanitary measures were taken to prevent epidemics. Within hours, water and electricity were provided. Thousands of loaves of bread and milk were distributed free for children and civilians. The Arab mayor of the city looked on with amazement at such humanitarian treatment. The Israeli told him, "Yes, we know. You would have tortured and starved us to death."

The Arab population, misguided, misled, and betrayed, is bewildered and pitiful. All their lives they were fed lies. An excellent example was witnessed by Israeli Arabs in Haifa. They were listening to the Arab version of the war's progress from Cairo: Tel Aviv is completely wiped out! Haifa refinery is on fire! But when they turned to look out their windows, they saw the refinery intact. So they turned on Israeli broadcasts which were giving people accurate, truthful developments every hour.

Here, we are working wholeheartedly for peace. There are no brass band parades, no terror, no oppression. The gates are wide open for everybody to move in both directions of the Old City, to meet relatives, old friends, to worship freely, and to trade. The Israeli are not bragging about their conquest. All they want is to prove that this is their home as much as the Arabs' and the Christians', and together they can beautify it and glorify it in peace.

There is a lot more, my son, I would like to tell you, but I'm tired. I've been at this letter almost a whole day. The urge to put it down on paper while the memory is fresh was very strong, and I'm glad I did it.

Love,
MOM AND DAD

*In a letter written on May 30, before the outbreak of war,
Chana Weingarten, a former Philadelphian, tells relatives
about the hectic preparations being made for war. Once
again it is apparent that it was the women's and children's
high morale and hard work that provided the necessary
backbone for Israel, while the male population prepared
to go to war to defend their country.*

May 30, 1967

DEAREST MIRIAM, IZZY, AND SYMA,

. . . Life here goes on as much as it can, although in a
different way. Everyone is busy in civil defense, either
digging trenches or fixing up shelters. Yesterday I went out
to the center of town, and near the supermarket I saw a
bunch of people crowding around an ambulance. Like any
other normal person, I went to see what happened and was
told that people were signing up to give blood. You have no
idea how wonderful the people are. Everyone is helping. In
the post office the high school kids are busy sorting mail and
delivering it. Even in the supermarket, kids are working to
help fill in the shelves. And then the boys in the schools,
elementary and high school, are busy digging trenches in
places where there are no shelters. Women are baking cakes
to send to the soldiers, and in general, there is a wonderful
cooperation from all. Even the children are helping—fixing
up the shelters, shlepping sand to fill in sandbags, cleaning
the shelters, and just everything. Everyone wants to do
something. Of course, our only wish is that we will not need
it, and everything will be okay.

Everyone is glued to the radio every hour for the news,
and even in school they stop every hour for the news. The

kids, of course, can't study too well, if at all. Meanwhile, my nursery school is still going on. Even the little kids feel something, since most of their fathers are not at home.

There are many students who have volunteered to work in kibbutzim where people have been taken and they don't have enough helping hands. University students have volunteered to teach in schools where teachers are away.

There's a nice story that I just heard. A very religious man from Bnei Brak was called up with his truck, and he was asked if he wanted to be mobilized or did he want to get paid for what he was doing. His answer was if he got paid, then he wouldn't be able to work on Shabbas, so he would be mobilized. On Shabbas, a Hassidic rabbi in Safed called his people in the middle of prayer, and they all went out straight from shul with hoes and started to dig ditches. The rabbinate has given their permission for work (essential) to be done on Shabbas, and there is no one who refuses.

CHANA

This letter, written by Joan Gottlieb to Rabbi Ralph Simon of Chicago, gives a moving account of the strained atmosphere before the Six-Day War. Her letter not only reflects her courage and dedication in preparing for the conflict, but also illustrates once again the unity and fervor among all the Israeli civilians to aid and contribute—in whatever manner possible—to the preservation of that small nation.

August, 1967

DEAR RABBI SIMON,

. . . Independence Day this year was a very quiet one, this being a year of recession and great unemployment. None of the governmental bodies was in the mood to spend much money on celebrations, most of them finding themselves in straitened financial situations. In view of the above circumstances, added to which was the spectacle of increased emigration of professionals to more affluent countries, people found little to celebrate about. The following morning, however, we were greeted over the breakfast table with the news that Nasser was sending troops to Sinai. At first no one paid too much attention, because everyone was sure it was a political maneuver aimed at pleasing Syria. It became apparent the next week that he was very serious, for it was then that Nasser announced that he was closing the Strait of Tiran. From that point onward, the tension in Israel continued to mount. It was then the people began to realize that in all probability there would be war. His announcement also signaled the beginning of large-scale mobilization, and overnight a good proportion of the male population disappeared from the streets of Israel.

This caused a good many problems, not the least among

them being the transport of goods. A small proportion of the population began to hoard, but most people bought only what they needed for the immediate future. When the owner of the local grocery store was called up, those people with cars offered to go to Tel Aviv and bring his wife sugar, flour, rice, or whatever else was needed. She permitted no one to buy huge quantities of food, so there was always enough for all. Our local post office was left with no one to sort and deliver mail except the postmaster, so the students from the local high school went there and voluntarily did the work. Every day one could see them walking down the streets, delivering mail. Teen-agers all over the country pitched in and did everything they could. They worked in hospitals, helped out in the kibbutzim, dug trenches, and did whatever they could wherever they were needed. These same youths who had been looked down upon as being superficial showed themselves to be as worthy as their fathers, who served during the war for independence.

On the home front we busied ourselves with readying ourselves for war. We prepared first-aid kits, dug trenches in our backyards, pasted strips of cloth over the windows to prevent the glass from flying in case they broke, readied black paper for a blackout, and painted the headlights of our cars black. I was also busy teaching English, at the local high school, but I can assure you that no one was in the mood to learn English. How could they be, when everyone's father or brother was away from home? As the days passed and nothing happened, the morale began dropping, and all the offers of help and letters of encouragement which began to pour in from all over the world helped cheer us up. The appointment of Moshe Dayan to the post of defense minister raised morale once again, for while we all knew that his stepping in would at that point make little difference in the military sense, he nevertheless served as the symbol that we needed. Monday morning everyone went to work as usual, but at a few minutes after eight o'clock, the air-raid siren sounded, and within a few minutes we heard the announcement over the radio that the war had begun. We spent a good part of the morning in the shelters, and the children kept up their spirits partly in order to swallow their fear. All of us were afraid, for none of us doubted what our fate would be if the Arabs won. Everyone knew that the Arab threats of raping the women and killing the men would be carried out to the last one of us, and more than one woman would put aside a nice sharp kitchen knife, "just in case." Yes, the Arabs had murder in their hearts, and we all knew it. Ramat Hasharon is only about eight miles from what was previously the Jordan border, and more than once I had stood on our second-floor balcony and looked at the Arab villages on the hills (the Hills of Ephraim) and wondered what would happen if—

Our house has two stories, and that afternoon, after having spent a good number of hours in the trenches in our backyard, we decided to move our bedding into the living room downstairs in order to be closer to the trenches in case there were further air-raid warnings. Thus far we hadn't seen any enemy aircraft overhead, but one could not afford to take chances. Sure enough, just after dark and just after we had put the children to bed, the whine of the siren pierced the silence and the darkness. We grabbed the children and ran, together with the rest of our neighbors, to the trenches. The night was pitch-black, except for the thousands of stars which shone overhead. There was no moon, this being the beginning of the Hebrew month, and not a light shone anywhere in Israel. Had it not been a night of war, we all would have felt a thrill of discovery and great pleasure at this unforgettable sight. The reality, however, was the fact that the distant thundering of guns to the east was joined by the sounds of shells whistling overhead and exploding a short distance away. Would one hit our house or even us, only ten meters away? Our son Michael, who is eight, understood what was happening and began to cry. Our younger children didn't quite know. Fortunately, however, nothing happened to us, and after the all-clear signal we were left in peace until dawn. The artillery pounding did not cease during the night, but this time it was we who were pounding them. It all came from the Jordanian town of Kilkillia, so when, after the war, Israeli forces blew up a number of houses there, I felt absolutely no regret. At dawn we were awakened by another sounding of the siren (this time it was a lone Iraqi bomber which had come to bomb Tel Aviv, but which bombed Natanya by mistake), but it was worth getting up at five in the morning to hear the news over the radio announcing the destruction of 430 enemy airplanes by our own force. The next days were filled with joy and exultation and with pain. The joy and exultation were for our salvation and for the victories of our armies, and the pain for the losses in life that we knew we were suffering.

The climax of these momentous days occured on Wednesday evening with the announcement of the liberation of the Old City. In a special radio news broadcast we heard a recording of the blowing of the shofar by the chief rabbi of Zahal at the Wailing Wall, moments after it had been taken. Everyone who participated, the rabbi, the dog-tired paratroopers, who had paid so dearly in their fighting, the announcer, we who sat in our darkened living rooms and listened, everyone was overcome with emotion. It was an unforgettable moment in a memorable week. The anticlimax is also worth mentioning. It was one evening the following week that the numbers of dead and wounded were announced. It proved to be less than most people expected, but it nevertheless left us speechless. Israel is a small country, and each one of our sons is valuable. All of us felt personally affected even though we might not have known any of the dead. Perhaps that is one of the advantages of living in a small country. One doesn't lose his identity here.

The war has ended for the time being, but the killing hasn't stopped. Only last week a neighbor down the street was killed during the shooting at the Suez Canal. He was a young man, an architect, married only a few years. He left behind a widow and two children, the older being only a little over two years old. We are in a state of limbo, of no peace and no war. This is the same state we have been in for the last nineteen years, but at least we no longer have "border settlements." Now it is Egypt, Jordan, and Syria who have them. What does the future hold? None of us knows at this point. We hope for the best, but neither the Arabs nor the Russians seem ready for peace in this area.

So these were just a few impressions of an ordinary Israeli housewife, of a Chicago girl faced with a reality far different than what I had ever imagined even in my wildest dreams. . . .

Regards,
JOAN

Ruth Bach, who was public relations manager of the Tel Aviv Hilton Hotel during the Six-Day War, wrote the following letter to her main office. In it, Miss Bach tells of the excitement and tension in running what was to become the nation's "newsroom." In spite of the loss of male personnel, blackouts, and the influx of news reporters and their equipment, the hotel survived to return to "business as usual."

TEL AVIV HILTON
July 19, 1967

DEAR L.,

On May 21, the hotel was still completely full. Even the lanais by the swimming pool were occupied, and many groups and individual tourists scheduled to arrive. . . .

Then the crisis started. The U.S. and other embassies advised their citizens to leave the country, and the tourist exodus began. Quite a few groups and individuals stayed on, determined to complete their sight-seeing tours as scheduled and many of them convinced that war would not break out.

"If they want me to leave, they will have to carry me out of here," stated an elderly tourist from the United States on receiving the embassy's circular letter.

Another lady, reluctantly packing her bags and getting ready to leave, came out on the terrace overlooking the sea as the sun was setting. "How deceptively peaceful it all looks!" she sighed.

At the same time, press, TV, and radio personalities began to arrive at the Hilton from all over the world to cover the crisis and waiting impatiently for "things to happen."

Meanwhile, mobilization was intensified, and most of the young men, as well as a number of girls, were called to the army. Those notified rushed directly from work into the army. A waiter, on entering the King Solomon's Grill from the kitchen with a full tray, received word that he was called up. He went over to his guests, put the tray beside the service table, called another waiter, and told them where he was going. "Hope to see you after the war," he added, smilingly, and off he rushed to join his unit.

Most of the hotel's male key personnel were drafted, too, which presented serious problems for the running of the hotel.

The top floors were closed, and guests moved down to the lower floors. The King Solomon's Grill Room and Chalim nightclub were closed, and all meals served in the Milk and Honey Coffee Shop and Snack Bar. The Coral Bar was kept open during the day, but at night, during the blackout period, the Chalim Bar was used instead.

With the general tension mounting, preparations for a possible outbreak of hostilities were speeded up. The hotel's air-raid shelter was equipped with all the essentials required for an emergency, including sandbags, fire-fighting and first-aid equipment, telephones, and, for the convenience of its occupants, tables, chairs, mattresses, blankets, hurricane lamps, refreshments, etc.

Press rooms were set up in the hotel's private function rooms and suites, additional telephones installed, and the hotel's Telex put at the disposal of the journalists, who availed themselves of this service around the clock. The hotel's telephone operators did an outstanding job handling hundreds of local, long-distance, and overseas calls twenty-four hours a day, and everybody was full of praise for the incomparable facilities and excellent and devoted service they received at the Hilton.

On June 5, early in the morning, war broke out, and at 8 A.M. the first air-raid alarm was sounded. On that day guests and staff moved into and out of the shelter no less than eight times, including three times during the night.

As soon as the alarm sounded in the city, guests were requested over the hotel's loudspeakers to proceed to the shelter. Elevators and electricity were shut off, but on every floor, staff members with flashlights led the guests by the service stairs down to the shelter. There was no panic at any time, and everything went off smoothly.

The shelter was buzzing with activity: Journalists and photographers were interviewing and shooting the people assembled there—guests, as well as staff. Commentators of the major TV and radio networks were holding onto the specially installed telephones and shouted their reports overseas—everybody trying to get ahead of his competitors in dispatching newsworthy items as fast as they came in.

Many distinguished visitors converged on the Hilton shelter: Mayor and Mrs. James Tate, of Philadelphia, paid a surprise goodwill visit to Tel Aviv and brought greetings of support from Philadelphia, Tel Aviv's "twin city." The ambassadors of Britain and Brazil with their wives had moved to the Hilton shortly before the war broke out. Barons Edmond and Alain de Rothschild with a French parliamentary delegation of about twenty VIP's arrived from Paris and found themselves in the shelter shortly after checking into the hotel.

Among the important press and TV personalities at the Hilton were Charles Collingwood and Mike Wallace of CBS, Saul Bellow (author of the best seller *Herzog*) , Winston Churchill of *News of the World* (grandson of the late

Sir Winston Churchill) , Charles Douglas-Home of the London *Times* (son of former British Conservative Prime Minister Sir Alec Douglas-Home) , Sidney Gruson, foreign editor of the New York *Times,* Cornell Capa, well-known *Life* photographer, and many others, representing all the major radio and TV networks, newspapers, and magazines.

One of them, *Life* photographer Paul Schutzer, did not join us at the Hilton shelter. He had used all his energy and influence (even appealed personally to his old friend General Moshe Dayan) to be assigned to an assault unit and was killed during the fighting around Gaza in the first hours of the war.

An American Peace Corps physician came to volunteer his services to help Israeli doctors. He and his wife had come to Israel for a reunion with their parents from Detroit, who had arrived a week before the war as tourists. "I would be glad to help out, but I do not think my profession is particularly useful just now. . . . I am in the electric sign business. . . ." the doctor's father told us while sitting in the carefully blacked-out Hilton Bar.

The bar became the meeting place for press, TV and radio people, high-ranking Israeli officers and other VIP's. Reports from the various fronts were discussed, unbelievable stories told, political discussions held, and predictions made. It all seemed like a dream, some of it like a nightmare.

There was never a dull moment at the Hilton: One day General Dayan was interviewed by CBS; on another David Ben-Gurion appeared for ABC, each company closely guarding their "secret." Commanders, generals (including General Odd Bull, head of the UN Truce Supervision Organization) , and other important military personnel went in and out of the hotel, lending additional glamor to the Hilton during these days.

The client we missed is Ahmed Shukeiry, head of the Arab Palestine Liberation Army, who one day before the war told the manager of the Ambassador Hotel in the Old City of Jerusalem: "Next week we will be staying at the Tel Aviv Hilton!"

One who deserves great praise for his indefatigable efforts in winning the war at the Hilton is the executive chef from Switzerland, Marcel Roth. With almost 75 percent of his kitchen personnel in the army, including the Israeli chef, he was left with one qualified cook to keep his department going. He was on duty from 6 in the morning until 11:30 at night, with the result that all the meals were prepared and served promptly and satisfactorily, and the 150 guests at the hotel hardly noticed the tremendous shortage in manpower. During the first two days Mr. Roth was kept particularly busy between cooking and running to and from the shelter. Once, down in the shelter, he suddenly remembered meat left in the oven, so, without a moment's hesitation, he ran back upstairs to the kitchen to rescue the roast. "No casualties," he reported happily after he joined us again in the shelter.

Mrs. Roth, the chef's pretty young wife, was as brave as her husband. Upon being advised, like all foreign nationals, to leave the country, she refused to go. "My husband decided to stay at his post, and I will remain by his side," she stated. Her only request was to be allowed to help us in any capacity she might be needed.

One of the busiest and most profitable departments during this period was the laundry department. With a drastically reduced staff, it had to cope daily with large quantities of laundry and dry cleaning, mostly from the journalists and camera crews traveling back and forth between the Sinai Desert and other fronts.

A total of 155 members of the Hilton staff was in the army, and although many of them are still "somewhere" on duty, we are happy to know that all of them are safe, although several of them have lost close relatives in the war.

RUTH BACH
Tel Aviv Hilton

A refreshing pause from the general topic of conversation during that critical summer of 1967 occurs in the following letters written by a young American girl, Diane Spevack. Miss Spevack, a senior at Ohio State University, was a volunteer in Israel. A vivacious and productive worker, she wrote many lively and enlightening letters to her family in Cleveland. Miss Spevack made many friends in Israel, and through her perceptive descriptions of her new acquaintances, we gain some insight into the character of the Israeli people.

MOUNT SCOPUS
August, 1967

MY DARLINGS,

Well, the avid volunteer is happily back to work on Mount Scopus with a pick and shovel, after five glorious days of roaming through the hills of Galilee. Oh, it was a tremendous adventure, traveling up and down those historic mountains, swimming in the Mediterranean Sea, the Sea of Galilee, the Tiberias Sea . . . seeing so much of this fascinating country. You can't imagine the genuine beauty of this land. It looks like untouchable scenery, painted in oils, from the sky to the earth, an incredible existence of nature's beauty.

Let me start from the beginning. Monday morning we all piled on the trucks at 5 A.M. These trucks are designed like buses with four rows of wooden board seats in the back. Each truck holds about forty to forty-five people. We were very crowded, because we had about ninety people, so you can imagine the discomfort of five days of bumpy roads on these trucks. Can you picture about forty people trying to

sleep on someone else's knee, rib, or elbow, whi.
around the curve of a mountain? Well, we did 1
what you call real group togetherness.

In Hebrew the trip is called a tiul. We had three p
with us from the Jewish Agency. Philip, who was the n
guide, about twenty-six or twenty-seven, was a real pist
He knew the Galilee like the back of his hand.

Our first stop was Daliyat el Karmil, a Druze village.
With its shops and handmade goods, it actually looked like
an Indian settlement. Our second stop was in Akko (Acre),
where we visited a museum, a sad reminder of Nazi concen-
tration camps. Actual photos of the victims and the camps
were the main displays. It was a devastating experience for
everyone. I felt so empty when I left, shocked at what I saw.
Although I had read books, seen pictures, and knew what
happened to 6,000,000 Jews, I suppose no Jew can fully
comprehend or accept that such a tragedy could ever happen to a people. Nevertheless, what took me in the most was
one display set in the center of the room, a large black case,
and in the center, the torn dress of a little girl of about five
or six. And beside that, a pair of dirty, holey shoes. That
was all. Oh, God, what an emptiness we felt! There are a
few of these museums erected in Israel. Yad Vashem is one
in Jerusalem.

In Acre we saw a fortress that was attacked by Napoleon
in 1799. Downstairs was a prison that was used for the
Haganah. Dayan spent some time there. This prison is now
used as a mental hospital. We spent Monday night in
Nahariya. We swam in the Mediterranean until about 3
A.M. Unbelievably fantastic! The town had an amusement-
park kind of atmosphere. The youth hostel where we stayed
was beautiful and reminded me of Camp Wise.

Tuesday morning we left Nahariya and drove to the

Lebanese border. We stopped for a while, took pictures, and talked with a few Arab shopkeepers (there are a few in our group who speak Arabic) , and then on into the Upper Galilee. We saw Joshua's tomb and climbed a fortress on the highest mountain, an unbelievable sight. On one side you can see Lebanon right behind, and on the other side is Syria. We drove up through the beautiful Syrian Hills, resplendent in color and exciting glamor. We passed Tel Hai, where we saw the memorial for Joseph Trumpeldor, a 1948 war hero.

We stayed the night in the youth hostel in Safed. Safed is a fantastic city, the oldest in Israel and one of the oldest cities in the world. It is a very holy city, and has thirty-nine synagogues, of which we visited two. The first was the Ashkenazi synagogue called the Lion. The Cabalists used to live in Safed. They searched through symbolism, trying to discover when the Messiah would come, and 200 years later the Hassidim came. Based on the teachings of the Cabalists, they pray facing the south, because of their position with Jerusalem. The bema and the arc in this shul are over 100 years old. The pictures on the bema, which are rarely seen, show historical Jewish incidents. In this shul, the Torah lies down. The second synagogue we visited was the Oriental Sephardic synagogue. Here the Torah is standing, and read in this way also. Torah in Arabic means mountain; isn't that interesting? The Torah stands here because of the position of the people to Moses when he brought the scrolls down from Mount Sinai. We also saw an exhibition at the Art Gallery by Safed's contemporary artists—Labkovski, Avniel, Amitai, and others.

We continued traveling to the northernmost part of Israel. We went into Kiryat Shmona, a small town of immigrants, and then to another small town, Metulla, and now toward Syria. We passed Kibbutz Myri Baroch, Kibbutz Dafna, and Kibbutz Dan. Dan was bombed during this past war. It is the most northern kibbutz in Israel, next to the Syrian border. We went into Syria. It was a strange, frightening, and yet exciting feeling, actually to be in Syria. We stopped in Baynas Springs about noon on Wednesday. We also stopped at a huge Syrian market. Surrounding us were mountains with many wide caves. Nearby was the Syrian army camp with blown-up tanks all about the roadside. With wide-open eyes, like children on their first day of nursery school, we wandered, observing the many religious Syrians dressed in long black robes and top hats with canes. A fantastic sight, with weird overtones. We also passed Kenitar village, the main army camp of the Syrian heights.

By this time we were all so tired from that truck—our behinds so sore, and bodies so dirty and dusty—we stopped for a three-hour swim in the sea. North of the Galilee Sea and over the hills, we were approaching Israeli territory. We passed the place that bombed Kibbutz Dan. Open mines were all over the sides of the road, covered by white cords. We passed small Baby Jordan River, and then on to Kibbutz Amiad which is mostly English immigrants. I wouldn't want to be on a kibbutz with 90 percent English. What's the purpose?

Wednesday night we stayed in a little paradise called Oma, a resort for conventions of different Israeli organiztions on the Tiberias River. The grass was so green, about three inches high, and glorious trees. We stayed in little cottages, and had *hot* showers for the first time in Israel. We slept outside on the grass. This was a heavenly place, certainly no place for volunteers. We left Thursday morning about 7 A.M. and went around the old eastern border of Israel, south of the Kinneret, by the Sea of Galilee. We stopped at a Roman amphitheater—Bet Shan. A very interesting story here: There used to be an Arab market over the top of this amphitheater, but it was shell-bombed and completely wiped out. The remains of this theater was found, and so it was rebuilt again. This was a beautiful and historic sight.

We stopped at Haifa Beach for a swim and lunch. There we toured an ancient synagogue from 527 B.C. There were large rocks surrounding the center of the synagogue inside. Artistic designs covered the walls. Then we were off to Afula and south to the Megiddo valley. Here eighteen cities have been built on top of this valley. Incredible!

Completely worn out, talked out, and sung out, the thought of getting back on that truck was almost unbearable. We longed for our home on Scopus. However, we were at least twelve hours from Jerusalem, so on we continued.

Thursday night we stayed in a youth hostel on the Jordanian border. We went into Genine, a small Jordan village, also called Shomone, from the Shomonites. It is a triangle of three towns: Shem, Nabbis, and Genine. When our truck stopped, mobs and mobs of Jordanian children crowded the back of the truck, trying to sell us goods from the market. These children are so beautiful, very dark, with big, haunting eyes. However, we were told not to buy anything. People all over the streets were selling things. They crowded around us, pulling at us. Because there was still an area of danger here, we had to say we were tourists, and not volunteers. As we left, many began to throw stones at our truck. It was frightening. This was the first time I had encountered hostility and hate, and the mood was quite obvious.

Friday we didn't make any stops. We drove straight back

to Jerusalem. It was an unforgettable trip. We came back to our hard work at Mount Scopus tired and with nothing but sleep on our minds.

By Sunday we were refreshed and ready again for the challenges of a volunteer.

Love,
DIANE

August 20, 1967

DEAR HEARTS,

Everything here at Mount Scopus is progressing so well. And I spent the most wonderful birthday of my life in Jerusalem, in the home of a remarkable family, who embraced me with love. Well, to the beginning of my adventure. For the volunteers who wished it, we were sent as guests to Israeli families for the Shabbas weekend. Well, I sure lucked out. I was Queen Esther . . . and Shu-Shan was Beit Hakerem, a suburb of Jerusalem. There I presented myself at the home of the Beinharts, and looking like a forlorn urchin, dirty, unwashed, "Please, before I introduce myself, can I have a shower?" Before the weekend was over, I had three showers and two baths, and everyone understood.

Mr. Beinhart is a dentist. His twenty-one-year-old son Shuky is a student at Hebrew University. A married daughter, twenty-five, is an accomplished artist, whose paintings grace the walls of their home. The twenty-six-year-old son is a dentist, now in Tel Aviv with the army. Sara, twelve years old, is a dark beauty—long black hair, big, flashing eyes, very intelligent, speaks a little English, and a ballet dancer.

Shuky, the twenty-one-year-old, is an absolute dream. He was my escort for the weekend. Anyway, Shuky is unbelievable. He wants to be a dentist, but he plays guitar, is building a speedboat, paints, has a fantastic personality, and is every girl's dream, I'm sure. The Beinhart home is like a mansion by Israeli standards—three floors, a family room, beautiful paintings displayed all over the house, and Shuky's original little tables and figurines. Their grounds are tremendous, with peach trees, apple trees, pears, plums. They grow all kinds of vegetables, have chickens in the barn, and have a flower garden, which I'm sure is the envy of the neighborhood.

The Beinharts were so warm and hospitable, and the dinner was *great* with soup, chicken, assorted vegetables, fruit salad, wine, and, for dessert, caffè cappuccino, and homemade peach pie. Well, you can imagine what happened to my skinny little tummy. Shuky translated to everyone (there were a slew of relatives over), about my home, my family, my university, my volunteer program. I showed them pictures of all of you and your column, Mom. I tell you, they're in love with my family, and I think that they really liked me, too.

Saturday, Shuky took me to see the Israeli Art Museum, the Knesset (parliament) building, new Hebrew University. Out to lunch in a Jerusalem café, and then an unforgettable tour of New and Old Jerusalem. What a day for a birthday! The best I've ever had! Saturday night Shuky had a birthday party for me. What an evening of unbelievable togetherness! All of Shuky's friends came over. Hardly any of them spoke English, and I spoke no Hebrew. But with song, dance, and that great international language of good food, we had a fantastic time.

Sunday morning, when I left the Beinharts, they gave the

little deprived volunteer hangers, soap, candy, and a few books to read on Jerusalem and Israel's history. I am invited there next week to meet the older brother. This I cannot wait for. BACK TO MY MOUNT SCOPUS. . . . Yes, the work is still hard. We work five days a week (no Fridays or Saturdays) . Working from 7 to 1:30 is hard, especially what we do, but we all work hand in hand. Everyone gets cut, bruised, stomachaches, from lifting the heavy rocks, but it's become our trademark. I have four black-and-blue marks, a few cuts, a sprained finger, six-day diarrhea (which is now two weeks old) . You just would not believe the destructions and shambles that are yet here. We have cleared a lot of it up. We have swept all the rooms in the old Hadassah Hospital and the old Hebrew University. We have scraped the plaster off the walls and ceilings, taken out all the broken windows, etc. Our volunteers from all over the world have so much in common, in sentiment and enthusiasm, so we are experiencing our love of being in Israel very much the same way, and together, and especially being here. Those words from the Psalm "If I forget thee, O Jerusalem" take on a new meaning.

I must tell you about yesterday. It was Tisha b'Av. About twenty of us got up at 3:30 A.M., and we walked to Old Jerusalem to the Wailing Wall. It took us a little over an hour and a half. I won't even try to re-create this experience for you, because there are no words. Walking there was beautiful, warm, historical, frightening, sensational. The Wailing Wall left me paralyzed. People were really crying aloud—praying, kissing and hugging the wall, and this at 4:30 in the morning. There were thousands of people, Hassidic Jews, little boys and girls, old men with tear-stained eyes, young women, sobbing and praying. We went to the wall. We kissed it and said our own personal little prayers. I don't know if mine was really a prayer. But I felt full of electricity, and I felt wholesome before that wall. We stayed there until about 5:30 and then went into the Arab village in Old Jerusalem for breakfast. We walked back to Mount Scopus and went to bed. The beauty and silence of the twenty volunteers who walked back yesterday morning as the dawn rose over the mountain is locked in my heart forever.

I'll write again soon. I do love Israel and being a volunteer so. I wish you were here to share it with me. Only for this am I sad.

Love,
DIANE

KIBBUTZ MISHMAR HA EMEK
December, 1967

DEAREST FAMILY,

Life on the kibbutz becomes more satisfying and soul-searching every day. Each little experience adds up. Each day more smiling faces and more friendly shaloms draw us into the intricate pattern of kibbutz life.

First of all I have met Rama, the most fascinating woman I have ever encountered. Her English name is Irma Lindheim. She is past president of national Hadassah in the United States, was a private student of John Dewey at Columbia University, and the only woman to study for a rabbinical degree at the Jewish Institute of Religion.

Her autobiography, *Parallel Quest,* gives the details of her life. At the age of eighty-one Rama vibrates with the spirit of adventure, a zest for life, and a love for people.

My roommate, Julie, and I talked with her for two hours—of home, Israel, Judaism, and life. She did most of the talking, and we sat with our mouths agape and our eyes sparkling with fascination. Here is a woman who has lived an exciting, happy, satisfying life—a life fulfilled with the hopes and ideals of a rare and remarkable individual.

Yom Kippur on the kibbutz was an unusual experience for me. The people here are quite antireligious. In fact, that's quite true of most of the people I have met in Israel. Here on the kibbutz, religion is looked down upon—almost scoffed at.

It is a difficult thing for me to understand and to accept, but their Judaism comes through the history of the Jews, their heritage, not God or religion.

All the holidays—especially Succoth, Hanukkah, and Shavuoth—are celebrated with great pride, but not at all religiously. They are historical holidays, a remembrance of *why* they [Israelis] are Jews and from where they came— but no such concept as *God* is involved. He simply does not exist.

It is a difficult way of seeing Judaism—and hard for me to accept. Nevertheless, Yom Kippur here was observed as a definite time for Jews to remember who they are today. However, there was no fasting. In fact, only twelve members in the ulpan and four volunteers fasted—and a few kibbutzniks who are recent members.

I fasted because I wanted to—and because I felt that even across the miles, I was closer to my family. I went to services Erev Yom Kippur with about ten other people in the ulpan to a small synagogue about ten miles from here.

It was a moving experience, and as I participated in the singing of some of the prayers that I knew, I felt that we were really "together" that night. A friend and I spent

Rosh Hashona in Beersheba and went to a small synagogue there. Amazing, there were mostly older people praying there. Where were the young people?

Succoth is tomorrow. The kibbutz will be bursting with joy and laughter. There will be a big party, entertainment, and a feast. People are busy decorating their succahs. This year I will really experience the true meaning of Succoth in the land of my people—and it will have a very personal touch for me.

Love,
DIANE

Early December, 1967

PEOPLE OF MY HEART,

Well, Kibbutz Mishmar Ha Emek (see . . . I can't even spell it in English anymore, because I think in Hebrew now) has almost succeeded in making a genuine little kibbutznik out of me. How will I ever be able, in just two weeks, to pick up my things and say shalom forever?

I have been promoted and am now working in one of the children's houses (two and a half and three year olds). When Sifra called me into her office and told me that my Hebrew was satisfactory for this age group, I was overjoyed. Anyway, it's quite challenging. I work with Ruthie, Rivka, Yadia. We feed these little enchanting midgets, bathe them, play, go for walks, and send them off to their parents at noon. I'm in paradise.

My relationship with my adopted parents, Daliyah and Eddie, is fantastic. How could I be so lucky to have been chosen by them? They are exciting, vibrant, full of life, with a real love for people. Just like us! Eddie helps me with my Hebrew lessons and makes me toe the line. I have also inherited two warm and loving grandparents. There is a special magic about Afriam, my grandfather. With him I have an intimate attachment, something I've never really had. Dad, you're so much like him, and though you may never meet him, I think that I've really brought the three of us together.

Of course, my real love affair—besides the romantic ones —is with my eighty-one-year-old Rama. She is the most inspiring, remarkable person I have ever met. She is a rare, sensitive, brilliant woman, whose courage, convictions, and ideals led her some forty years ago to the land of her people. She has written *Immortal Adventure* and *Parallel Quest,* and she remains one of the giants of the world. Despite her great stature, she is a warm and affectionate friend. She calls me her "special little girl." I have basked at her feet, as she recounts to me her experiences as a young girl from a wealthy and affluent German-Jewish assimilated family; as a young matron going into her international career as a Zionist, what motivated her, the people who influenced her (Rabbi Stephen Wise, Ussishkin, Henrietta Szold). She is truly a rare individual, endowed with the finest qualities of intelligence, awareness, affection, integrity, and love for life and people. She has devoted much time to me, and as for me, I feel as if I'm the disciple of a great teacher and philosopher. Saturday our two-hour session will be devoted to discussing motivation in teaching—what I can expect of myself when I teach. We will also discuss her method of discovery teaching in Jewish history. Sometimes we just sit and talk about people, life, love, ideals, family. Other times we choose a topic, and I actually bone up to keep pace with her agile mind.

Did I tell you about Joseph? He is twenty years old, from Bombay, India, and wants to settle in Israel on a kibbutz. He speaks English beautifully, since he went to a private English school since he was ten. He's quiet and shy, but with a deep perception into what is going on about him. He is a very bright boy, searching for something that he didn't find in India. He comes from a wealthy, high-class family, but somehow, in India he could not find his identity as a Jew. He decided to come to Israel and a whole new world has opened up to him. Emigration from India is very small, but I admire him for having the courage of his convictions to leave a comfortable family and a country. But this is not uncommon in Israel.

Bela Traub, my little Russian roommate, and I have a very comfortable friendship. Amazing! At first we couldn't communicate at all, and now she speaks to me in Hebrew and I respond in English, and we're both doing great.

Yona and Yaacov, the French couple from Morocco, live next door. They're short, chubby, pug-nosed, with curly brown hair—an adorable couple.

Gagy, from Argentina, speaks only Spanish and Yiddish, but somehow we get along fine.

French Shimon is a guy I adore. He's the cutest little bug with blond curly hair, big blue mischievous eyes that twinkle as he rattles off in French.

And the others, Shlomo and Rafael from Spanish Morocco, are interesting characters, with a culture that is quite different from ours. David, from Paris; Sima and Mickael from Paris; and a charmer from Bolivia. Last week we had a great Tower of Babel on a bus. A few of us decided to hitch into Afula to shop. On the bus ride home, we turned that bus into an uproar from Afula to the kibbutz. We had an exciting seven-way conversation going in the back of the bus in English, Spanish, Hebrew, French, and Bela even threw in a few sentences in Russian. Oh, we were fantastic. Everyone on the bus went wild. We never had more fun. Everyone on the bus was laughing and saying, "Ma zeh? Ma zeh?"

I have many more favorite people on the *kibbutz*—Yona and Odid. Yona works in the Mitbach Yelodim. She is twenty-four, a Yemenite Jew, as petite and beautiful as you could find. Everyone here has an interesting story. She was almost sold into marriage as a slave in Yemen when she was fourteen. Her parents were in favor of it, but she ran away and was later brought to Israel by the people who adopted her. They live on another kibbutz.

The weather has gotten very cold, freezing in the early mornings and nights. There is no heat here, nothing like my warm room at home. Anyhow, the rains come down quite often, and the kibbutz has equipped us with the proper clothes. It's funny, the clothes they give us just to keep warm, and we all look like immigrants. Funny I should say that. Probably about half of us are.

And now I'm going to give this letter to Dolek, the postmaster and one of my favorite people. I'm mad for him. He's seventy-one years old, six feet tall, and he hugs and kisses me with each mailing. Such is life in Mishmar Ha Emek, but I'll be home soon with a lifetime of memories, and a heart full of love.

Your wandering pigeon,
DIANE

This letter was received by Mr. and Mrs. Menachem Kolari of Flushing, New York, from their daughter Nitza Rothstein, who lives in Israel with her husband and children. Full of excitement and suspense, Mrs. Rothstein's letter describes her reactions to the Six-Day War. She, too, was amazed at the strength of the civilians' spirit and labors.

June 18, 1967

DEAR MOM AND DAD:

This letter was long in planning, but I have written it a thousand times in my mind. So here goes—get comfortable, turn off the TV, take candy and enjoy.

I cannot tell you how much we appreciated your letters and especially your attitude in standing by us in an hour of grave and difficult decisions. I knew the decisions we made wouldn't be completely condoned by you; but we had to make them, and you were wonderful in responding as you did. It seems that at an hour of crisis "all of us Jews" are the greatest—besides which I knew you to be the greatest of all (not prejudiced at all).

Now down to brass facts. First of all, let me tell you that we have been privileged to live and go through an experience that for the rest of our lives we will have to thank God for. To be Jews is a privilege, to be a Jew in the United States is a privilege; but to be a Jew in Israel at *this* time is a supreme privilege, and this is it in a nutshell.

About five weeks ago it all started. We have got used to living with odd incidents, but upon Nasser's dismissal of the UN troops the realization came that this was something different. Events happened in a speed which gave us little chance to think. A week later the streets started emptying of people and cars. Offices started missing people. We realized that there was quiet mobilization.

And we poor citizens and residents slowly became politicians and strategists, hawks and doves, and, of course, volunteers. People around us—mostly Americans and diplomats—started talking about leaving the country. Mike and I never really discussed it—and we continued from day to day knowing exactly how the other felt. Each of us discussed it individually with strangers asking us why are we staying, and each of us answered and formed his own feelings about it. For me, personally, the question of leaving never came up. I have been through it before, and it was a fact of life. But of course, now I am a mother and a wife, and it's quite different. Mike had his own ideas—at first he said that I should leave with the children while he stayed. This was out of the question for me—and of course, I don't think he meant it, too. There is a curious factor in time of danger that makes each of us feel indestructible and that *we* will *not* get hurt. This enables us to go through all sorts of things.

Abba and Ima were with us, and we were happy to be here—and never said a word about what we should do. Finally, on Sunday night before the war, which started on Monday, Mike and I decided to sit down and discuss the matter and, once we decided, not to mention it again. We sat up half the night and looked at the problem most realistically, down to the horrible details of "what if we get hurt," etc., etc. We decided that there are very few issues in life that are so clearly black and white—and that we think are so important—and we have found such an issue, and if we don't do whatever small part we have to, to stand up and uphold that issue, and if we run away from here, the personal consequences will be worse than the mere fact of dying. So we prayed and put the whole thing in the hands of God, luck, and fate, and we decided to stay. By the way, having a choice makes it much more difficult, and don't forget all the little children around us, Navah's and Danny's friends, who had no such choice. I would just like to add, so you don't think we are such heroes, the fact that on Monday morning, sitting in the shelter and listening to the shelling around us, all the theoretical discussion of the night before went out the window, and I was looking in my mind for a way to get the kids out. But thank the Lord I didn't have to use it. All the above that I wrote is just a small sample of the way we felt and thought so that you can understand. I promise to tell you all when I see you.

Now to the more energetic happenings. I mentioned the mobilization—within a week most of the civilian population was in the army. The cars and trucks and buses were mobilized; offices and factories and stores were emptied of employees. It was an eerie feeling. It is hard to understand that this army is made up of 80 percent civilians, and life in the cities and around the country is at a standstill. The civilians all gathered with magnificent spirit to help each other. The buses were not running properly, so each of us with a car picked everyone on the road up, so they can get to and fro. Besides two days of panicky food shopping, all remained calm. Each man who was *not* taken to the army was crying and begging to be accepted—and if not, they went to kibbutzim to help pick fruit and work the fields or help dig trenches. My meshuggane husband had his name on every volunteer list in the country, and when he was given some job to do, he was in seventh heaven. He helped on some programming for the army—and a few days before the war he was taken into the civil defense unit, and he was in charge of our area of houses around pituach. And of course shvitzing like mad.

I was with a group of women volunteers to send packages to the army and to help those who are left behind—pregnant women without husbands, information, deliveries, etc. I also took a first-aid course—the kind they give for what you do in case of major mass emergency—whom you evacuate to hospitals first, etc., etc. Just to give you an idea, while the instructor was talking, women fainted down the aisles like flies, and that was just from the talking. To boot it all, I had been quite sick during that time with a severe case of tonsillitis with joint pains, and of course, there were no doctors available because they were in the army. (But that passed, and I am *completely* fine.)

As the week grew nearer, the war hawks grew more restless. In our house we had nightly war games. We drew maps and assigned soldiers and planned attacks till the wee hours of the night. You'd be amazed what experts we all became, but that was the only way we could pass the tense time while listening to news.

Mike and another friend kept insisting that they wanted to go to Kfar Hanasi, which is on the Syrian border, to help in the kibbutz work. (A kibbutz near the house was not good enough for them.) So, finally, on Monday morning we set out to go up north. The children went to school, Abba went to the office, and Ima stayed home to baby-sit. Mike and I and another couple went out at 7:30 in the car on our merry way. We naturally put the radio on. Lovely music was playing and we singing happily on our way. All of a sudden there was an announcement on the radio in Hebrew: "Zahal spokesman announces heavy fighting at the Sinai border." Period, end of sentence. I was the only one in the car who understood Hebrew perfectly, and I quietly said, "It started!"

Mike became white (ears red), and the silence was deafening. We were just before Natanya, so immediately we decided to go back; after all, we do have children, and we really are not irresponsible. We decided to drive into Natanya, where we have a friend, so we could at least call home and get some information. We pulled into the main street of Natanya, and there were police everywhere, cars stopped in the middle of the road and people congregated in halls. I told Mike, "What's going on here?" and he said, "Probably some accident." We went to our friend, and of course, we heatedly discussed the situation. Two minutes later we heard a siren, an all-clear siren. We stupid idiots were riding on our merry little way during an alert. We folded our feet and ran to the car and "flew" home. When we got home, Ima was already on the verge of fainting from worry (by the way, she had a gallbladder attack that day). We called Abba to tell him we were home, and we started working. The kids I left in school because of previous instructions by the civil defense not to converge on the schools, and they would take care of the children. Mike reported to his civil defense station, and I went shopping for food. Later, with my friend, we drove to the volunteer station to help them with shopping for first-aid stuff and for blackout paper. Afterward we blacked out our house, in between running to the hall (which was our shelter) during alerts, filling sandbags, and digging a trench near the house.

Abba called from town and said he had no way of getting home, and would we come and pick him up? I left a friend with Ima, and Len (our friend) and I went into town to pick up Abba.

That was at 11 o'clock, approximately. The radio was

calling the units in code to report to their assigned stations. Like roaches and ants, people came out on the roads, responding to the army call to go to their point of departure. It was amazing how fast they gathered about, as if they were going to get something for free. P.S. This letter stopped for a week, and I seem to be stuck.

Well, we fixed our makeshift shelter and stayed at home. Ima was sick. As the sounds of shelling came to my ears, I became frantic about the kids and thought maybe we should get them out. But I really appeared calm, but knew that there was no way or need yet. Of course, we had a rough night, but by the next day the news of the victory started to come in, and although we didn't believe it yet, it relieved us.

By the third day we knew, and every time we heard a plane in the sky, we ran out to look and were completely confident that it was always our plane. That's really the greatest feeling.

About Jerusalem, Mike wrote to you, and words really are so poor to describe our feelings. Well, God was good to us, and we were honored to be here. Mike's frustration at not being able to do more and help more didn't quite subside completely, but I can tell you, it sure felt good just to be here.

We are now touring the country in the new territories. Of course, we go only where we can get a pass, and it is fascinating. Jerusalem, the Old City, is so beautiful, like an unreal movie set.

We are trying to go to Jericho, Shclem, etc. Next week and the week after, Mike is probably going with Mekoroth group to Suez, Sinai, Tiran Strait, etc.

This Wednesday we might just go to El Arish to "view"

the troops—seriously, Varda's husband is finishing his tour of duty, and we are invited to the ceremonies.

Hopefully, we'll go to Syria soon, and by then it will be November and time to leave. We'll be terribly sorry to leave the place. Somehow this country grows under your skin forever and ever, and that includes those people who were *not* born here.

Well, that's all for now. I'm exhausted, and I can't possibly cover everything. . . .

Love,
NITZA

The excerpts which follow are taken from letters written by Gloriann Grayman and her brother Burt to their parents, Mr. and Mrs. Henry Grayman. Covering a period from May 23 to June 24—from the weeks of preparation, "Israel is one big coiled spring. . . ." to the end of the war, which Gloriann describes as "both a miracle and a nightmare"— the letter draws the reader into their active lives. Gloriann is a graduate student, and Burt is a senior at the Hebrew University, as well as vice-president of the National Student Union in Israel.

1967

May 23: Last night Nasser closed the Strait of Tiran to all cargo bound for Israel. He knows Israel's present government is more reluctant than Ben-Gurion's to become involved in war. . . . The university is almost empty now, and it is difficult to concentrate on my studies. I must venture to say that Egypt will be so badly defeated by the Israeli forces that she ought to be wise and not start anything. The U. S. State Department advised American citizens to leave the Middle East. However, as you can feel in your heart, this is no time for Gloriann and me to pick ourselves up and leave. I still hope that the war will be averted and that the tension will pass. Please do not worry, as your children will be safe.

Love,
BURT

May 25: Everyone is involved in the present political situation, and they are quite tense. We were all evacuated from the university, and all teachers and students were sent home. Because the school is so close to the border, the authorities do not want to assume responsibility under present conditions.

GLORIANN

May 26: I must say that the reaction to the present situation here is really fantastic, as the Israeli soldiers ran to their bases without waiting to be called while foreign students, women, and children rushed to the Jewish Agency, the university, and local government offices to volunteer. The people are very relaxed and secure, and their spirits are very high. Nobody knows exactly what to expect, but everyone is confident that Israel will meet its needs bravely.

BURT

June 2: Volunteers keep streaming into Israel every day. . . . People are needed on the kibbutzim since most of their members are sitting on the borders in the army. I am keeping busy taking a four-hour first-aid course and also spent several hours the day before helping clean the shelters in my apartment house, and today I baked a cake for the soldiers. . . . Everyone is pleased with the appointment of Moshe Dayan as defense minister. A new coalition which includes all the parties was formed, and everyone is overjoyed. Actually the whole country is in a working-together spirit, and people have been just wonderful.

GLORIANN

June 4: As much as it seems to the world that Israel is one big coiled spring, just waiting to snap, surprisingly enough, many people are spending the weekend at the seashore. The weather was hot but dry, and I spent the weekend here in Haifa with a girl friend who was called into the army about ten days ago and is serving as an officer in the Haifa army hospital. . . . Today I spent a hard day at the office preparing explanatory material and requests to petition and demonstrate for PEACE IN THE MIDDLE EAST to all the National Unions of Students. . . . There is no doubt that the unity expressed by some of the free world with Israel has been rewarding, and the volunteers and contributions from so many Jewish communities have been very comforting and portray a bright side of the picture. But if only Nasser could be convinced of the need for peace!

BURT

June 7: I am now in my apartment after spending most of the last forty-eight hours in our shelter, including sleeping there two nights. . . . I was sent to Katamon, very near the border, to help the families of Oriental immigrants living there to prepare themselves in case of attack. Many are quite hysterical. It was my job to quiet them and give them a sense of security. About 11 A.M. the air-raid sirens went off. I quickly got them into shelters and walked around with the civil defense group for quite a few hours while the shelling was active on the border. I was perfectly calm. About 5 A.M. I returned to my apartment building and went down to the shelter of our house, where everyone was calm and just wonderful. We played Scrabble and cards, listened to the radio, sang to the children, and told them stories. The shelling continued all through the night, as did the rockets and Stens. I must say I was a bit frightened by this time but did not show it. We had electricity all the time, as well as water and food, and morale was high. We stayed in the shelter for two days. We had some pretty heavy losses and many wounded soldiers. My heart hurts for every boy we lost.

GLORIANN

June 8: Today is Jerusalem Day! Flags are flying all over and everyone is out on the streets wishing one another mazel tov! Some people have already gone to pray at the Wailing Wall. Jerusalem was hardly damaged except for some bullet holes here and there on the borders, but we paid a very heavy price in blood. We lost many soldiers, and we have many wounded.

GLORIANN

June 9: Tamar Golan (a friend) just arrived together with forty foreign correspondents on a special military plane. I arranged to meet her in order to assist the correspondents in getting around to meet the right people and to get to the right places. I learned a hell of a lot the last few days, most of it really shocking, which I will relate to you when I see you this summer, I hope. About 800 homes and buildings were hit by mortar shells but not too badly while most of the people were in shelters during this time.

BURT

June 11: I think it is all over now. The shooting has finally stopped in the north, and our border has been quiet since Wednesday. . . . I must say this past week has been both a miracle and a nightmare. The accomplishments of our army cannot be explained logically—it has to be accepted as a miracle. Claire received a phone call from Hadera from someone who found a note on the street from Moti when he was passing through the city. The note read that he was alive and healthy and asked the finder of the note to phone Claire. She was overjoyed! . . . It has been quite hectic at Hadassah Hospital, Phyllis tells us. Because of the shelling, all the babies were delivered by the nurses, with dentists serving as anesthetists, and every doctor was in the operating room, from gynecologists to foot specialists, for work on the soldiers. . . . I pray that we will now see a new era of peace in the Middle East.

GLORIANN

June 17: On Shavuoth over 200,000 people went to the Wailing Wall. There is only one road open through Mount Zion, which is guarded by hundreds of soldiers, and it is now quite safe to go. . . . Everyone who fell in battle is somehow known to everyone around us, and it is a terrible thing. Thus, no one in this country will be ready to give back the Old City or any of the defense areas we now have. The number of Arab refugees total almost a million, and their own people refuse to take them. Those who left the Old City for other parts of Jordan were turned away and are now wandering about in the Gaza . . . It is said that the stench is awful, as the Egyptians refuse to bury their dead.

GLORIANN

June 24: There are over 3,000 volunteers here—Jewish youth from all over the world distributed in all the kibbutzim. Israel is now in a state of overflow of volunteers, as there is no room for them in the kibbutzim and no need for them in the cities. WHAT IS NEEDED THOUGH IS A NICE ALIYAH FROM THE STATES, OF PROFESSIONALS, etc., who are willing to live here. . . . Israel has managed to stir up something in three days of war which the Zionist movement has been unable to do in forty years. The important thing now is to try to hold the interest of the youth—I am not sure how.

GLORIANN

The following two letters were written by Mrs. Yohanan Beham to Lillian Margolin. Mrs. Beham brings alive the excitement and tension during those critical days in June and tells of her apprehension for the safety of her son, a paratrooper in the armed forces. The second letter, written one month later, gives Mrs. Beham's view of the war from the perspective of one whose loss is indescribable. Her poignant appeal for a continuing faith and belief in Israel reflects that nation's deepening dedication to peace.

JERUSALEM
Friday, June 9, 1967

DEAR LILLIAN:

Our air force has really set a very bad example. Now Yohanan thinks the civilians can do no less and is determined to reopen the museum two days after the battle of Jerusalem—at least the unharmed parts—which means unpacking and replacing every item in the place. When I offered to help, he said that the job was under control, and I should tackle the next one—to relieve the anxieties of our friends abroad by a nice, long, reassuring letter.

Well, I have learned at least one lesson—in times of war one does not say, "I cannot," so I'll try to convey something of the thoughts and feelings of the last four days (the *facts* you must have by now from the newspapers and radio).

The last two weeks have been as close to heaven and hell on earth as I shall ever know. The weeks of waiting were perhaps the worst, preparing for a war one did not want and hoped would not come. Shelters, medical first-aid kits, supplies of water, and sandbags to fill—but mostly the agony of waiting and knowing that every minute we waited meant greater danger to our soldiers if we did finally have to fight. The weeks of waiting were filled with fear and foreboding; with feelings of special tenderness for our young; with incidents of such amazing thoughtfulness and gentleness; of such wonderment at the *softness* of our army —examples: Our daughter Shosh was assigned to a foreign news photographer (*Time-Life* magazines) , and in addition to acting as his translator and girl Friday, she took messages from boys at the front to their families, which she phoned through at night (the photographer was killed a day later) . Another example: When an elderly woman came to the army to say her only son had been called up and she was alone and afraid, a girl soldier was sent home to stay with her "for the duration." Could this be the army in the international press these days?

During the battle for Jerusalem, we knew the terror of war with terrible intimacy. In our street there were six direct hits, our children's apartment was hit, and I cannot tell you what a bullet hole looks like over the crib of our only grandchild.

For my own reactions, I have the kind of nerves that turn themselves off in time of danger, and then when it is all over, my relief turns into streams of tears. Yohanan spent the time when most people were in shelters chasing between the house and the museum, where some thirty secretaries and guards were bedded down in the shelters. They did a most remarkable job of packing into the shelters every single item in the museum, but no one had thought of food. So Yahanan scavenged the blacked-out, closed-down, eerie city for food. One day they ate white cheese; another he found salami (great fare for the two pregnant women who were there) ; another time it was felafel. I went over with him one night, having baked a cake, to keep up the morale with all the games like chess, checkers, Scrabble, jigsaw puzzles, etc. about the house. It is a ride I shall never forget—pitch black; no lights on cars, of course; no moon; not a glimmer of light coming from any window. Shells bursting in every direction, machine-gun clatter—in a night studded with stars and the smell of honeysuckle mingling with burned gunpowder.

It is amazing how still the inside of a room can be when, just outside one's windows, the sounds of war shatter the eardrums. There were hours when I could not hear the mortars for the thoughts that clamored in my head—for once I was secretly glad that two of my children were in America, feeling that if we were wiped out here, a remnant would remain to carry on. My thoughts were constantly abroad with family and friends, sensing their concern for us, comforted by the knowledge that all of you were with us by that invisible atmospheric thought process that beams courage and confidence in time of stress. The need for action was such a compulsion that I, who detest housework, cleaned out every closet and cupboard in the house and mechanically added twelve inches, in the wrong direction, to a sweater I have been crocheting.

Yesterday we visited the Old City. We visited the old university on Mount Scopus and the Hadassah Hospital and the Wailing Wall. A week ago, visiting the Old City was a gag, a joke you made about the extremist political parties that advocated such measures, something one admitted to being a fantasy, a childish, foolish, impossible yearning—"don't be silly; grow up; face reality," you told yourself. And there we were, threading our way through winding alleys, down a steep staircase, the stone steps of which showed the 1,900 years of use they had seen, into a court-yard, long and narrow, of which one wall is about two stories high, of huge stone boulders, an occasional clump of weeds growing out of the cracks and crevices—this is the remaining relic of the Western Wall of the Second Temple destroyed when the Jews were dispersed from Israel.

Although we are not at all religious, we followed the tradition and custom of writing on a small scrap of paper the names of our children, folded the paper into a tight little roll, and stuffed it into a crevice between the stones. And suddenly I realized how significant and symbolic that action was. Suddenly I knew how enormous was this day for Israel, Jerusalem made whole. I knew that we had writhed these days in the birth pains of a new era for us. We had added a chapter to the Bible. And someday, 3,000 years hence, when our descendants read how the Israelis took on four armies, twenty times their number, and vanquished them in sixty hours, someone will get fancy with the interpretations and claim the word "hour" in "those times" does not mean the hours in our time and the recorder of the saga wrote "his version," etc., etc.

The soldiers in the Old City stood about, shy and proud, smiling, modest. Somebody said, "Chag sameach [Joyous holiday]" and a boy replied, "Sameach meod [Very joyous]." Everyone murmured, "Mazel tov," with unashamed tears glistening in the sunlight. The words "kol hakavod" (all honors to you) brought a nod or smile. They were so young, eighteen, nineteen years old, and they looked ten feet tall to us as we looked up to them from our own new height of nine and a half feet.

One is never bored with nothing to do in Israel—but now the prospect of things to do is overwhelming (of course, after the last week "overwhelming" is just a new reality) . In the museum alone, Yohanan is worried with the bill for repairs to the buildings, which were already burdened with debts. Not a single object in the museum has been harmed —and the damage can be repaired.

What cannot be repaired ever are the lives we lost—as yet the total is unknown, but after all, numbers do not measure the pain and loss this means to those of us who have this to bear. This letter goes off while we still wait for word about our son who is a paratrooper. Most of us are still in shock, staggered by the enormity of our good fortune, this miraculous victory when we only dared hope for survival and a lessening of tensions. . . .

Warmest regards,
Bee

July 6, 1967

Dear Lillian:

Today is Shloshim, the thirtieth day after the death of our Yuval. He was killed in the Old City of Jerusalem on the second day of the battle which united the city.

To us, he was a son—Yohanan's only son to a father who was the only remaining member of his family to survive Hitler's Germany . To me, he was a stepson, an extension of his father, a relationship acquired when he was already a young adult.

In many ways Yuval was like his father, his quiet confidence, his proud reserve, his intelligence more profound than clever, his love of sports and music, his varied interests from radio ham to what are the Russians reading these days, his code of ethics and values, his profound commitments and responsibility to his country's cause.

Yuval and his wife, Mickey, suited each other well. They

planned and shared their lives generously with love for each other and their child. Unlike his father, he and Mickey planned to have more than the one son he left, our one-year-old Alloni. When friends asked me "How is Alloni?" I frequently replied, "Oh, he's lovely, but his parents are really wonderful," because never have I seen two young people so ready, so eager, so delightful with parenthood. They enjoyed living—and life was beautiful and full for them.

A part of each weekend, when Yohanan was in town, they shared with us dinner sometimes or a Friday evening after-dinner visit to talk politics or shop, to hear a newly ac-quired recording or make a tape, to share the baby's newest development, the latest wisecrack about town or some overly rich dessert. Saturday morning tennis, a dip in the pool, our dog and the baby learning about each other, friends to share the leisure hours of the three generations of Behams, who, the rest of the week, rarely had an hour to spare from the pursuit of professional duties.

Yuval was well established in his chosen career in the Defense Ministry. More than most of us, he knew why he fought and died.

Yesterday, for the first time, I wandered within the walls in the streets of the Old City. It was a revelation at once hypnotic and repellent. Dirty, smelly, noisy, sleazy, teeming with life. Ancient stones haunted by the accumulated ghosts of centuries, the aura of the past as much in residence as the boiling cauldron of humanity that so frequently in its his-tory has boiled over but never evaporated. If one were to designate a time, place, and spirit that was today, yesterday, and always, its name would be Jerusalem.

But just as Moses yearned for the Promised Land he never entered, so would I, also, have lived out my time on the threshold of the Old City before I would sacrifice a single man to conquer it. We are no heroes or martyrs, nor do we have Abraham's calling or faith. Though Jerusalem is ours by the lives of our children, they fought not for land, nor religion, nor even honor. Survival—lechayim (to live).

I pray we shall not dissipate what we have paid for so dearly—and for the strength and wisdom to live up to the cause for which Yuval died.

You ask, What do we need now? Yes, dollars; even more: heads, hands, and hearts—but of a special variety. Not those who haven't found themselves elsewhere and want to try again, not those who come with personal conditions for staying. But those who are ready to take what is here and add to it, including the frustrations, inefficiencies, shortcomings, limitations, etc. We want well-adjusted people who have no reason for leaving where they are, business people, who don't expect to get rich but are interested in using their skills to build a sound economy, professionals who can raise standards and not demand standards; you know what we need maybe better than I do—you see what we have. Today my cabdriver was as rude as before the war; three days ago he was driving a tank. I asked him to pick up some soldiers on the road. He thanked me for them. When I said it was I who should do the thanking, he laughed. Then the soldiers compared the notes they'd received from schoolchildren (everyone had at least one), and one of them said, "I'm glad they teach them that we will look out for them—and better they should learn to write letters than to show them fear." There were five soldiers in the car: One was a professional, one a mechanic, the taxi driver, and two simple laborers. The laborers serviced aircraft; the professional led university students. There wasn't a grain of class consciousness; everyone would lay down his life for his officer—"he was always in front of me." We lost the highest percentage of officers to men in any known combat. Our Yuval's friends tell us, the men stood and fought and *advanced* after every officer had been killed, in the face of bunkers, on ground foreign to them. They took the Old City with terrible losses—and cried at the Wailing Wall. Can I ever again try to impose my standards of politesse on such as these? This generation need never feel inferior to the exploits or accomplishments of their parents. Will we ever live up to them?

Shosh was home for a night. She stood at my door and suddenly said, "Hey, today is six months I'm in the army!" "Mazel tov," I said, "you haven't done so badly: started and finished a war, tripled the size of the country—" Shosh replied, "Wel-l, three times nothing isn't much . . . but at least you can see us on the map!" She lost three classmates and her driving teacher, whom she liked very much. Can we ever think of them as children again—and they are still eighteen, nineteen only?

I will spend the summer within the circle of my family. I am grateful for your thoughts and concern for us.

All the best,
BEE

CHRONOLOGY

1897   Theodor Herzl called the First Zionist Congress, which declared publicly its intent to resettle Israel.

1909   Tel Aviv, the first all-Jewish city, was founded.

1914   At the outbreak of the First World War the Jewish community numbered about 85,000.

1917   On November 2, the British government issued the Balfour Declaration, which was a statement of sympathy with the Jewish Zionist movement and pledged support for the establishment in Palestine of a national home for the Jewish people. This was later confirmed in the mandate of the League of Nations.

1922   On July 24, the League of Nations issued its mandate for Palestine.

1947   In November 29, the General Assembly of the United Nations adopted a resolution calling for the establishment of a Jewish state in the land of Israel. Israel's Proclamation of Independence stated that Israel would:

> rest upon foundations of liberty, justice and peace as envisioned by the Prophets of Israel. It will maintain complete equality of social and political rights for all its citizens, without distinction of creed, race or sex. It will guarantee freedom of religion and conscience,

of language, education and culture. It will safeguard the Holy Places of all religions. It will be loyal to the principles of the United Nations Charter.

1948   On May 15, the day that the British mandate terminated and a few hours after the proclamation of Israel's independence, the armies of Egypt, Jordan, Syria, Lebanon, and Iraq, with Saudi Arabian contingents, crossed her frontiers at several points.

1949   During the first half of 1949, after about seven months of intermittent fighting, separate general armistice agreements were concluded between Israel and Egypt, Jordan, Lebanon, and Syria. Iraq and Saudi Arabia did not sign one.

1949   On May 11, Israel was admitted to the United Nations.

1956   Egypt began strengthening her military bases in the Sinai Peninsula and the Gaza Strip; the formation of a unified Arab command led the Israeli army on October 29 to destroy the Arab bases in the Sinai Peninsula. After one week of fighting the objective was achieved.

1966   At the end of the year the permanent population was about 2,660,000.

1967   On May 22, after increasing tension and hostilities, President Gamal Abdal Nasser of Egypt announced the Egyptian blockade of the Gulf of Aqaba. A little more than one week later Nasser and King Hussein of Jordan had signed a mutual defense pact which aligned the Arab nations against Israel. On June 5 war broke out—and a week later Israel's brilliant victory had gained for her the respect and admiration of the world.

GLOSSARY

Several words which appear in this book are either Yiddish, Hebrew, or colloquialisms. The following is a list of them with brief definitions—based on their use in this text.

Aliyah	Denotes the Jewish emigration to Palestine.
Avodat hutz	Refers to work done outside the kibbutz.
Bamidbar	The Book of Numbers.
Davened	Prayed.
Esrog	A type of citron fruit.
Galut	A Hebrew word denoting the position of the Jewish people deprived of their homeland and scattered among other people. It is also used to imply the persecution of these Jews by communities in which they live.
Gan	A yard or garden.
Hahshara	A term denoting the special agricultural training for immigrants coming to Israel.

Halutzim	Plural of halutz, or pioneer. It is the name given to the young Jewish men and women who went to Palestine between the two world wars to build the Jewish homeland.
Haverim	Plural of haver, or male co-worker or comrade.
Haverot	Plural of haverah, or female co-worker or comrade.
Kashrut	The Jewish dietary laws.
Kibbutz galuyot	Literally, the ingathering of the exiles. Refers to the gathering of the Jews of the Diaspora in the state of Israel.
Lulav	A type of fruit.
Mashgiach	The supervision of kosher food.
Olim	Those who emigrated to Israel.
Pituach	A development or design with regard to planning.
Sabra	A person born in Israel.
Shabbas	Sabbath.
Shomer hamayim	The guard of the kibbutz water tower.
Siddurim	Plural of Siddur, or Prayer Book.
Succah	The hut traditional to the Succoth holiday.
Tanach	The Bible.
Yahrzeit	The memorial day or memorial event after one year commemorating a specific event or occasion.
Yishuf	Literally, settlement. Refers to (1) the Jewish community in Israel or (2) the Jewry of any given country.
Zva Haganah	The underground Jewish resistance forces.